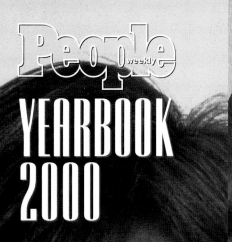

People weekly

YEARBOOK 2000

The
Year in
Review
1999

STAFF FOR THIS BOOK

EDITOR: Eric Levin

SENIOR EDITOR: Richard Burgheim

ART DIRECTOR: Anthony Wing Kosner

SENIOR WRITER: Jill Smolowe

CHIEF OF REPORTERS: Denise Lynch

PICTURE EDITORS: Lynn Levine, Evie McKenna

DESIGNER: Scott G. Weiss

CONTRIBUTING WRITERS: Alfred Gingold, Helen Rogan

COPY EDITOR: Lance Kaplan

OPERATIONS: Daniel J. Neuburger, Barbara L. Scott

Special thanks to Alan Anuskiewicz, Michael G. Aponte, Jane Bealer, Will Becker, Robert Britton, Betsy Castillo, Steven Cook, Orpha Davis, Nancy Eils, Tom Fitzgibbon, Brien Foy, Margery Frohlinger, Susanne Golden, George Hill, Joshua Himwich, Suzy Im, Rachel Littman, Eric Mischel, Ali Namvar, James Oberman, Stan Olson, Stephen Pabarue, Helen Russell, JoanAnn Scali, John Silva, Céline Wojtala

A division of Time Inc. Home Entertainment
1271 Avenue of the Americas
New York, NY 10020

PRESIDENT: Stuart Hotchkiss
EXECUTIVE DIRECTOR, BRANDED BUSINESSES: David Arfine
EXECUTIVE DIRECTOR, NON BRANDED BUSINESSES: Alicia Longobardo
DIRECTOR, BRAND LICENSING: Risa Turken
DIRECTOR, MARKETING SERVICES: Michael Barrett
DIRECTOR, RETAIL & SPECIAL SALES: Tom Mifsud
ASSOCIATE DIRECTORS: Roberta Harris, Kenneth Maehlum
PRODUCT MANAGERS: Andre Okolowitz, Niki Viswanathan, Daria Raehse
ASSOCIATE PRODUCT MANAGERS: Dennis Sheehan, Meredith Shelley, Bill Totten, Lauren Zaslansky
ASSISTANT PRODUCT MANAGERS: Victoria Alfonso, Jennifer Dowell, Ann Gillespie
ASSOCIATE LICENSING MANAGER: Regina Feiler
EDITORIAL OPERATIONS DIRECTOR: John Calvano
BOOK PRODUCTION MANAGER: Jessica McGrath
ASSISTANT BOOK PRODUCTION MANAGER: Jonathan Polsky
BOOK PRODUCTION COORDINATOR: Kristen Lizzi
FULFILLMENT MANAGER: Richard Perez
ASSISTANT FULFILLMENT MANAGER: Tara Schimming
FINANCIAL DIRECTOR: Tricia Griffin
FINANCIAL MANAGER: Robert Dente
ASSOCIATE FINANCIAL MANAGER: Steven Sandonato
EXECUTIVE ASSISTANT: Mary Jane Rigoroso

Special thanks to Emily Rabin and Jennifer Bomhoff

HARDCOVER ISBN: 1-883013-85-2
ISSN: 1522-5895

We welcome your comments and suggestions about PEOPLE Books. Please write to us at:

PEOPLE Books
Attention: Book Editors
PO Box 11016
Des Moines, IA 50336-1016

If you would like to order any of our Hard Cover Collector Edition books, please call us at 1-800-327-6388 (Monday through Friday, 7:00 a.m.–8:00 p.m., or Saturday, 7:00 a.m.–6:00 p.m. Central Time).

PRECEDING PAGE (from left): While **CHER** rebounded to the top of the pop charts with "Believe" and **MIKE MYERS** proved that his Austin Powers alter ego still had plenty of shagadelic allure at the box office, talk show host **MONTEL WILLIAMS** went public with his painful and heroic battle against multiple sclerosis.

PRECEDING PAGE (FROM LEFT): CHER (IPOL); MIKE MYERS (GEORGE LANGE/CORBIS OUTLINE); MONTEL WILLIAMS (PHOTOGRAPH BY MICHAEL O'NEILL); THIS PAGE: RICKY MARTIN (PAUL EMPSON)/CORBIS OUTLINE); POKÉMON (IMAGE COURTESY NINTENDO OF AMERICA, INC.); FOLLOWING PAGE: COLUMBINE (GARY CASKEY/REUTERS); JENNIFER LOPEZ (STEPHANIE PFRIENDER/CORBIS OUTLINE)

68 With a killer swivel not uncorked since Elvis, **RICKY MARTIN** jolts the pop world.

86 Pushing Furbies, Elmos and Cabbage Patch Dolls into the attic, **POKÉMON** rules.

26 Colorado's **COLUMBINE**
rampage leaves 13 dead
and a nation shaken.

CONTENTS

In an eerie echo of JFK's brief presidency, John and Carolyn Bessette, 33, spent a thousand days together as husband and wife.

JOHN F. KENNEDY JR. & CAROLYN BESSET
LOSTINTHENIGH

John F. Kennedy Jr. was America's renegade Prince Charming: a pampered political scion with the temperament of a lovable underdog; a dashing hunk with a beguiling lack of vanity; an A-list celebrity who was happiest walking unrecognized among the people. When his Piper Saratoga II crashed in the ocean off Martha's Vineyard on July 16, killing Kennedy, his wife, Carolyn, and her sister Lauren Bessette, Americans took the tragedy personally. They'd known this only son of Camelot from birth; now, unfathomably, at 38, he was gone. "John seemed to belong not only to our family," eulogized his Uncle Ted, "but to the American family."

On July 20, police divers searched for the wreckage of JFK Jr.'s plane.

Kennedy, who had logged 300 hours aloft since earning his wings in 1998, was authorized to pilot only under visual flight rules, which is to say, by the naked eye.

FINAL FLIGHT

Despite poor visibility at his Vineyard destination, Kennedy was cleared for takeoff. At 8:38 p.m. he lifted from a New Jersey runway, climbed to 5,600 feet, then began the 40-mile passage across ocean waters toward the Cape, where family members were already feting his cousin Rory and her fiancé, Mark Bailey. Within five hours, the wedding festivities would become a wake.

Three days after the plane's disappearance, the Kennedy clan, forming a protective circle around Ethel (center), still waited for the bodies to be found.

The first personal clue to be pulled from the waters on July 17 was a piece of Lauren's black luggage with her business card in a clear ID pocket.

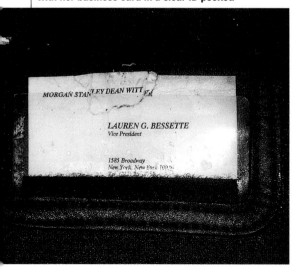

MORGAN STANLEY DEAN WITTER

LAUREN G. BESSETTE
Vice President

1585 Broadway
New York, New York 100.

On July 21, Senator Ted Kennedy witnessed the retrieval of his nephew's body.

SUMMER MOURN

After the nation awoke on July 17 to the heartbreaking news that Kennedy's plane was missing, Americans could think or talk of little else for a full week. Shock gradually gave way to grief as the five-day search effort drew to a close and the Kennedys and Bessettes laid their loved ones to rest.

Fans erected a shrine outside John and Carolyn's apartment, where they flocked to grieve (top).

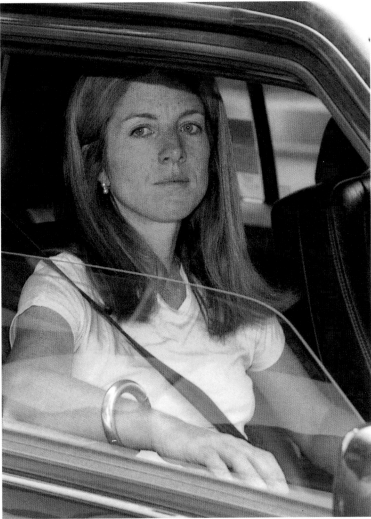

Caroline Kennedy Schlossberg, 41, provided a profile in stoic courage as she orchestrated her beloved brother's funeral and a subsequent memorial service.

As 17 members of the Kennedy and Bessette families stood on the stern of the Navy destroyer *Briscoe,* the ashes of John, Carolyn and Lauren were scattered over the sea off Martha's Vineyard.

SoulMates

He squired a string of celebrated beauties, from Sarah Jessica Parker to Daryl Hannah. But when Kennedy married Carolyn Bessette in 1996, his days as a Lothario came to an end.

MS 109 PT

Carolyn and John cruised off the Cape in 1995 in a craft christened to honor *PT-109*, his dad's famed World War II gunboat.

He called her Kitty Cat; she called him Mouse. Despite all the media attention, they regarded New York City as their playground in 1997.

John and Caroline (at the Kennedy Compound in 1963) were the first children to occupy the White House this century.

ROYAL WATCH

No matter what the occasion, John Kennedy Jr. attracted the camera's eye, providing an image that memorably marked the moment. A sort of natural wonder, he fit in anywhere. His ease stemmed from the self-reliance, grace and kindness that he'd learned from his mother Jackie. Once, in an effort to discourage young John's thespian ambitions, she cautioned, "You can either be or you can act." Kennedy's greatest artistry was that, despite the ever-present lens, he always chose to *be*.

Three-year-old John Jr.'s salute at JFK's November 1963 state funeral left history an indelible image.

Welcomed with a two-minute standing ovation, Kennedy galvanized the hall with his introduction of his Uncle Ted at the 1988 Democratic National Convention in Atlanta.

PEOPLE's Sexiest Man Alive in 1988, Kennedy displayed his athletic magnetism with ease on the Cape in 1997.

Despite his penchant for privacy, Kennedy did a cameo playing himself on *Murphy Brown* (with Candice Bergen) in 1995 when *George* first hit the newsstands.

PEO
PLE'S
PEO
PLE

Here are the saucy, sartorially interesting folks who lit up our lives—and pages—in 1999

ASHLEY JUDD When her single mom, Naomi, and big sister Wynonna first started burning up the country charts in the 1980s, 15-year-old Ashley played Cinderella, cleaning out their tour bus for $10 a day. Now, at 31, Ashley reigns. Her revenge thriller, *Double Jeopardy*, proved box office gold and burnished her screen image as one beauty who prefers vengeance to victimhood.

JULIA ROBERTS
Audiences simply cannot get enough of her mega-watt smile. As canny a woman as pretty, Roberts, 32, is Hollywood's highest-paid actress and in 1999 also seemed to hit romantic pay dirt (see page 74).

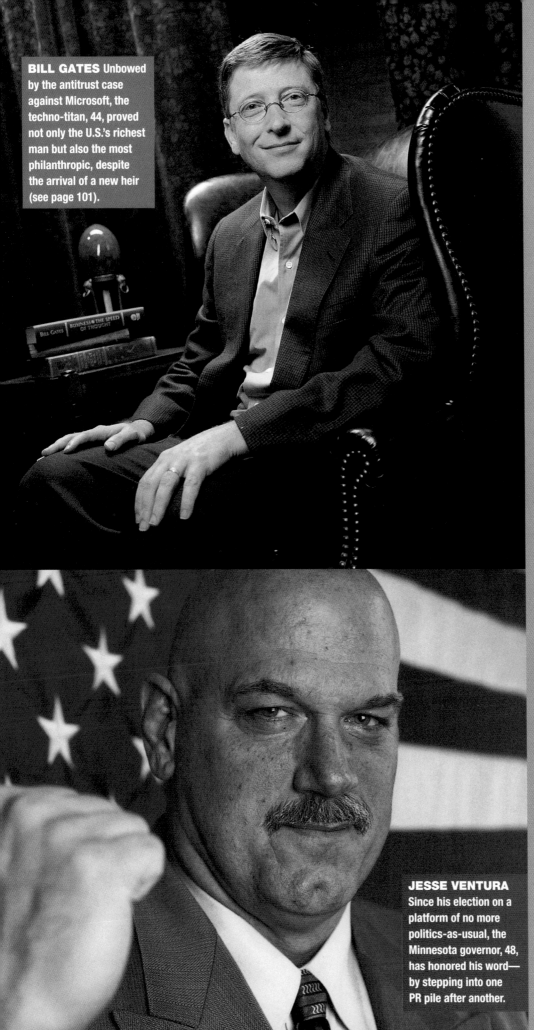

BILL GATES Unbowed by the antitrust case against Microsoft, the techno-titan, 44, proved not only the U.S.'s richest man but also the most philanthropic, despite the arrival of a new heir (see page 101).

JESSE VENTURA Since his election on a platform of no more politics-as-usual, the Minnesota governor, 48, has honored his word— by stepping into one PR pile after another.

17

BEN AFFLECK His rumpled allure, mischievous smile and wicked sense of humor offer "a unique combination of all-American kid and sexy bad boy," says Jerry Bruckheimer, producer of Affleck's summer smash *Armageddon*.

NICOLE KIDMAN Her erotic turn onscreen in *Eyes Wide Shut* and her nude appearance on-stage in *The Blue Room* excited fans, but she claims not to get it: "I wish I were two inches shorter and had that Sophia Loren look."

PEOPLE'S 50 MOST BEAUTIFUL PEOPLE OF 1999

Ben Affleck, *26, actor*

Jennifer Aniston, *30, actress*

Christina Applegate, *27, actress*

Burt Bacharach, *70, composer*

Evan Bayh, *43, U.S. senator*

Jessica Biel, *17, actress*

Cate Blanchett, *30, actress*

David Boreanaz, *29, actor*

Benjamin Bratt, *35, actor*

Tom Brokaw, *59, news anchor*

Josh Brolin, *31, actor*

Sandra Bullock, *34, actress*

Andrea Casiraghi, *15, Monegasque noble*

Daljit Dhaliwal, *36, news anchor*

Taye Diggs, *28, actor*

Jenna Elfman, *27, actress*

Emme, *35, model*

Joseph Fiennes, *28, actor*

Toland Grinnell, *30, sculptor*

Emmylou Harris, *52, musician*

Lauryn Hill, *23, musician*

Kate Hudson, *20, actress*

Jonathan Jackson, *16, actor*

Stephan Jenkins, *34, musician*

Derek Jeter, *24, baseball star*

Melina Kanakaredes, *32, actress*

Nicole Kidman, *31, actress*

Queen Latifah, *29, rapper/actress*

Lucy Liu, *30, actress*

(continued on following page)

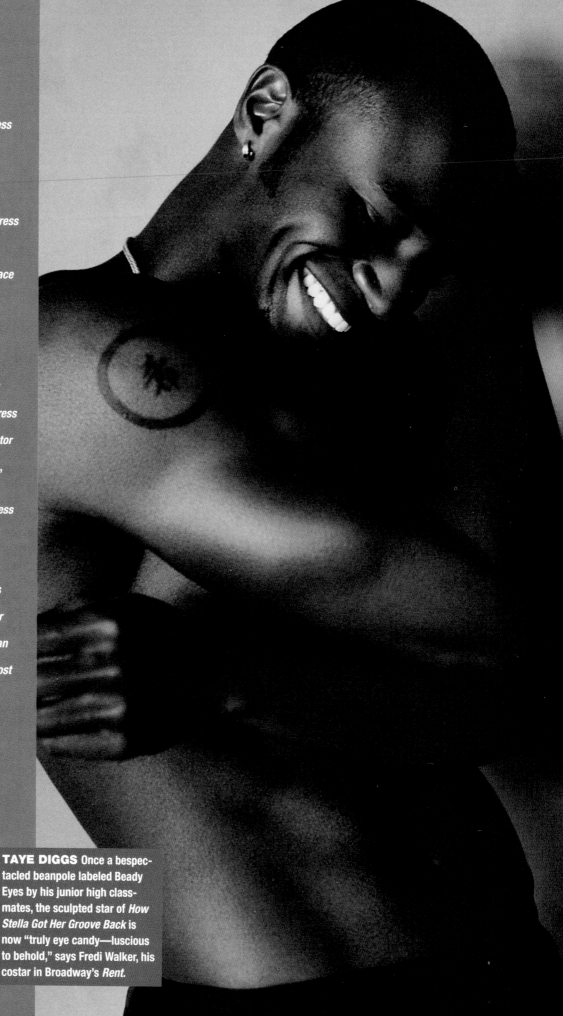

TAYE DIGGS Once a bespectacled beanpole labeled Beady Eyes by his junior high classmates, the sculpted star of *How Stella Got Her Groove Back* is now "truly eye candy—luscious to behold," says Fredi Walker, his costar in Broadway's *Rent*.

JENNIFER LOPEZ This Bronx-raised Puerto Rican's Rubenesque derrière became the subject of watercooler admiration and op-ed debates after she steamed up the screen with George Clooney in *Out of Sight*.

BEST DRESSED

PEOPLE'S BEST-DRESSED PEOPLE OF 1999
Candice Bergen, *53, actress;* Sophia Loren, *64, actress;* Camryn Manheim, *38, actress;* Ricky Martin, *27, singer;* Gwyneth Paltrow, *26, actress;* Brad Pitt, *35, actor;* Julia Roberts, *31, actress;* Diane Sawyer, *53, TV host;* Will Smith, *30, actor;* Catherine Zeta-Jones, *29, actress*

WILL SMITH donned wild, wild leather for the Grammys.

JULIA ROBERTS enchanted in her Vivienne Tam skirt.

CATHERINE ZETA-JONES sparkled in her flirty Versace.

DAVID ARQUETTE indulged his inner child on *Letterman*.

MADONNA looked scary in unmellow yellow on VH1.

ADAM SANDLER reveled in his grungy frat-boy image.

W O R S T   D R E S S E D

PEOPLE'S WORST-DRESSED PEOPLE OF 1999

David Arquette, *28, actor;* Mariah Carey, *30, singer;* Lisa Nicole Carson, *30, actress;* Cher, *53, singer/actress;* Val Kilmer, *39, actor;* Madonna, *41, singer/actress;* Nick Nolte, *58, actor;* Caroline Rhea, *35, actress;* Adam Sandler, *32, actor;* Shania Twain, *34, singer*

24

PEOPLE'S SEXIEST MEN ALIVE, 1999

Richard Gere, *50, actor;* Kevin Richardson, *28, pop star;* The Rock, *27, wrestler;* Jack Ford, *49, TV anchor;* Chow Yun-Fat, *44, action star;* Greg Payne, *22, model;* Michael Carricarte Jr., *31, philanthropist;* Lou Montulli, *29, Internet mogul;* Oded Fehr, *28, actor and émigré;* Ricky Williams, *22, athlete;* Po Bronson, *35, author;* Jesse L. Martin, *30, newcomer actor;* Alex Penelas, *37, politician;* Tim McGraw, *32, country singer*

KEVIN RICHARDSON With his limpid eyes and chiseled chin, this 6'1" Backstreet Boy (who met his secret sweetie while playing a Ninja Turtle at Disneyland) has a grown-up charisma that sets him

Fully 70,000 mourners turned out on April 25 to honor the 13 dead and to share their collective horror and grief.

Another Massacre in a School Jolts the Nation

A deadly rampage in Colorado by two young misfits leaves a trail of 13 dead bodies and a lifetime of lingering nightmares

Once, the word "columbine" summoned images of the blue-flowered plant of that name that garlands the Rocky Mountains. No more. Since the April 20 carnage at Columbine High School in Littleton, Colorado, which left a dozen students and one teacher dead and 23 wounded, the word has come to symbolize both the random terror that stalks America's schools and the determined fight that communities are mounting to reclaim those halls.

For four tense hours, Dylan Klebold, 17, and Eric Harris, 18, held the suburban Denver school under siege, firing guns and tossing pipe bombs, before fatally turning their weapons—two shotguns, a handgun and a semiautomatic rifle—on themselves. Administrators, teachers and students could take pride in the heroic selflessness demonstrated by many that fateful day. Several teachers put their own lives at risk when they rushed through the halls, yanking students out of harm's way. As Troy Manuello, 27, a member of the physics department, put it, "I got into the profession so I could have an impact on young lives—not so I could save them."

In the wake of the senseless slaughter, the backgrounds of Klebold and Harris were scrutinized for tell-tale warnings. Much was made of the fact that in the socially stratified microcosm that is Columbine, both seniors had belonged to a loose grouping of black-coated social outcasts known as the Trenchcoat Mafia. Both had also been arrested in 1998 on minor charges of criminal mischief. But no matter how their pasts were parsed, the two boys seemed more typical than problematical. Each had done well in Little League; both held after-school jobs in a pizza joint; both came from intact, two-parent homes.

The school, meanwhile, was shut down for a $1.2 million makeover to obliterate visible signs of the tragedy. Alterations were made in the tone of the fire alarm system, which had rung nonstop that day. To enhance security, 16 surveillance cameras and additional lighting were installed. Students were required to wear ID badges. And a "safe room" was established where kids and staff members could consult with one of the two mental health counselors added to the payroll. The school was reopened in August, except for the library, scene of the worst carnage. Even so, the scarring seems irreversible. In October the Columbine toll reached 14 when the mother of a 17-year-old girl, who had been left partially paralyzed in the rampage, went to a pawnshop and killed herself with a handgun.

In groups, the students were led from the school to waiting buses.

"I saw it!" said Diwata Perez (right) with Jessica Holliday.

Coming Back the Hard Way

Patrick Ireland no longer recalls most of what happened that day. But people who were glued to their TV sets during the unfolding drama remember vividly the moment when the wounded Ireland flung himself out a library window into the arms of rescuers. What viewers didn't know at the time was that Ireland, 18, had taken a bullet in the frontal lobe of his head and another in his right foot while aiding an injured friend. The 4.0 student spent his summer at a rehabilitation hospital, fighting his way back from a mute, partially paralyzed state. Once he stood a good chance of being valedictorian; now doctors caution that normal brain function has been interrupted, and further recovery will come slowly. Ireland, who says "I hate to lose," intends to fight—and Columbine students aim to help him win. Not long after returning to school, he was named homecoming king.

A Conflicting Tale of Devotion and Faith

According to original reports, one of the killers put a gun to junior Cassie Bernall's head. "Do you believe in God?" he demanded. "Yes, I believe in God," the 17-year-old responded firmly. Then the gunman shot her in the head. "There was a reason that Cassie died, and that was because she loved the Lord," said her father. "This was her mission." Cassie (inset) had been active at the West Bowles Community Church, and after the bloodshed her parents, Misty and Bud, honored her in a book, *She Said Yes: The Unlikely Martyrdom of Cassie Bernall.* Some investigators subsequently questioned the Bernall story and suggested that the student who had been pressed about and affirmed her belief was, in fact, Valeen Schnurr, 19. Though she suffered 34 pellet bullet wounds, Valeen survived and is now a freshman at the University of Northern Colorado.

A Battle to Get Back to Normal

"Before this, I would look at somebody in a wheelchair and feel sorry for them," says Sean Graves, 15. "Now I feel like congratulating them for surviving in the first place." Graves has been confined to a wheelchair since bullets tore through his stomach, damaging nerves that control movement in his legs and feet. On May 3 he regained feeling in his left foot, enabling him to move about for short periods with the aid of a walker. Though he returned to school in the fall, his attention remains focused on regaining his strength and coordination. "If he doesn't want to do something, it's difficult to nudge him," says his father, Randy, a computer-security engineer. "But if it's something he's interested in, he's like a bulldog until he's conquered it."

Unfriendly Fire

Bye-bye sugar and spice, as the Queen of Nice,
Rosie O'Donnell, blasts Tom Selleck on gun laws

Tom Selleck—part of the "I'm the NRA" ad series putting warm celeb
faces on the National Rifle Association—discovered what it's like to
come under fire, and in a most unlikely place. Visiting *The Rosie
O'Donnell Show* to chat up his new film *The Love Letter,* the actor
got ambushed by its normally congenial hostess. Dubbing herself
Miss Un-NRA, O'Donnell, 37,
demanded to know why his
organization is "against the reg-
istering of guns." Selleck, 54,
responded, "I am not a spokes-
person for the NRA." "You have
to be responsible for what they
say," retorted O'Donnell, who
since the Littleton, Colorado,
tragedy had been calling for laws
to make it harder for minors to
get guns. "This is absurd," said
Selleck. The next day, O'Donnell
sounded more like her usual self.
"I strongly do apologize to him
personally," she said. "But I
do not apologize for my feelings
about this issue."

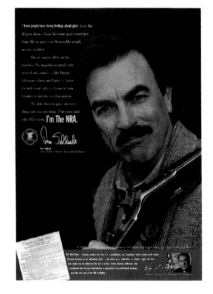

The Fight of His Feisty Life

Talk host Montel Williams
publicly acknowledges and
faces a formidable foe: MS

Montel Williams is ordinarily so full
of swagger that he titled his 1996 autobiography *Mountain, Get Out of My
Way.* But one cruel day in August, the
TV talk show host could barely move
his feet. While making his debut as a
movie director on the New York City set
of the drama *Little Pieces,* Williams, 43,
was forced to lean heavily on his actress
wife, Grace, just to hobble around.
"The pain just kept getting worse,"
recalls Williams. "I said to Gracie,
'Baby, you have got to get me out of
this room now, because I need to cry.'"

At an emotional press conference,
Williams disclosed what had driven him
to tears: He has multiple sclerosis, an
often debilitating neurological disease
that afflicts some 350,000 Americans,
including Richard Pryor and Annette
Funicello. For nearly 20 years, says
Williams, he has suffered from occasional blurry vision, stiffness and achy joints,
but had shrugged it off. "I was lifting
weights, I was running, I was in great
shape," says the strapping ex-Marine,
who scoffed at a doctor's suggestion 12
years ago that he might have MS. "How
could I be sick?" Then, in March, ex-
cruciating pain led him to Dr. Michael
Olek of the Harvard MS Center in
Massachusetts, who confirmed the diag-
nosis. "I came home and told Gracie,"
recounts Williams. "I said, 'If you want,
you can leave me, because I'm not going
to be the man you married.'" Grace,
35, scoffed at the thought, responding,
"There are a lot of people who need
you." She was referring also to their
children, 4 and 6, and his two older kids,
10 and 15, by a previous marriage.

"The hardest part Montel has with this disease is not having control," says wife Grace (with him in August).

Before long, he was back to his defiant self. "I'd talk to the pain," says Williams. "I'd say, 'You can go away now. You've made your point.'" He revealed on his show a couple of years ago that he'd faced down such a situation at 19, when he had a double mastectomy because of a lump in his chest that was later found to be benign. "I hope that Montel keeps working forever," says David Lander, the MS-afflicted actor who played Squiggy on *Laverne & Shirley,* "so people with MS can see it doesn't have to be crippling." Williams has a good chance. In his relapsing-remitting form of MS, bouts of pain come and go, often years apart. And although there is no known cure, his symptoms are generally controllable. Going public, says Williams, was an important step toward conquering his fear—and helping others. "God picks different people to do different things," he says. "I will run my mouth about this."

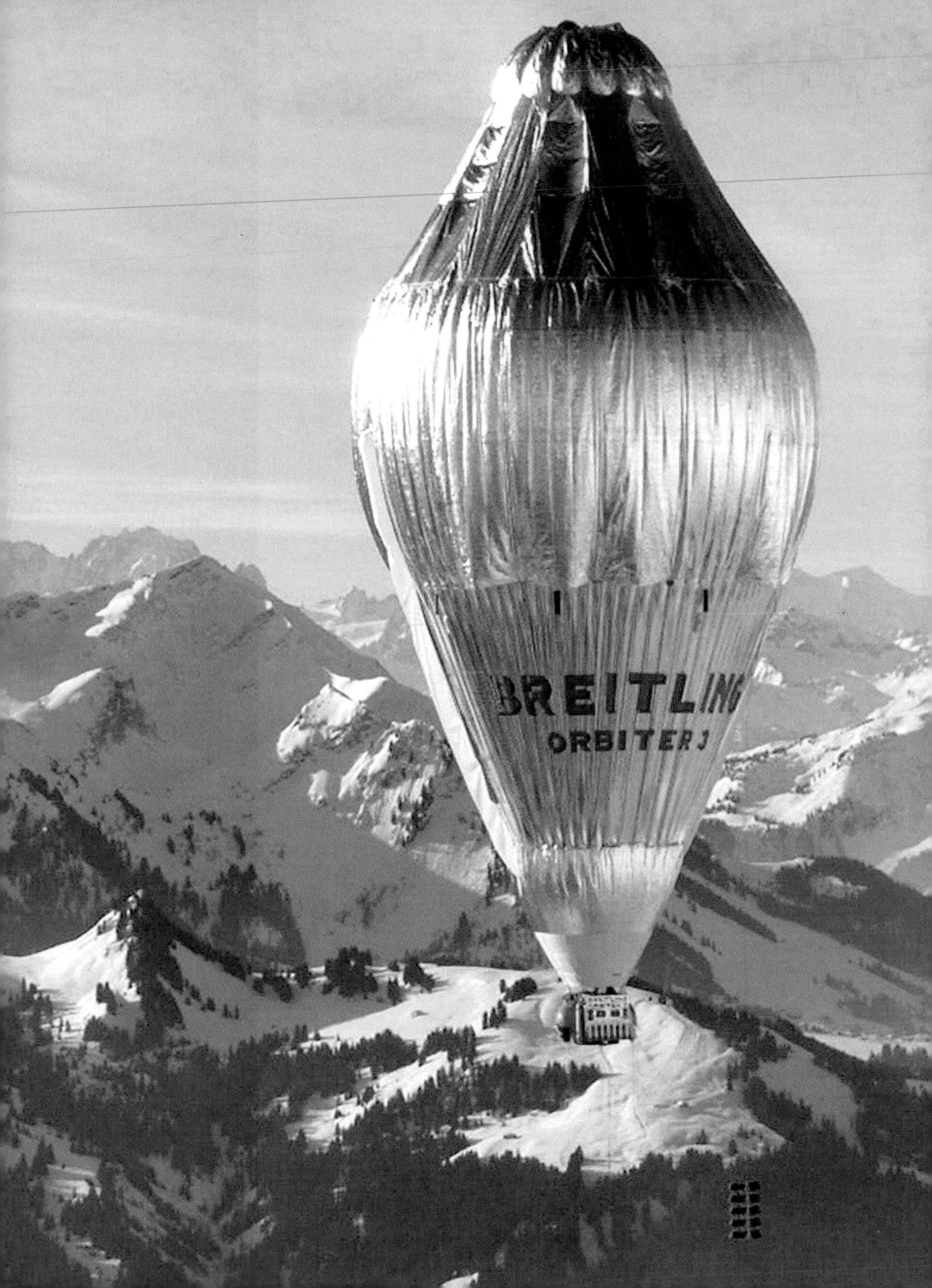
BREITLING
ORBITER 3

Round the World in 20 Days

Two brave balloonists attain a goal that had defied and killed others before

Over the years, more than a score of balloonist teams have tried in vain to become the first to circle the globe nonstop. So what was remarkable about Bertrand Piccard of Switzerland and his British partner, Brian Jones, was not only that they did it but how easy they made it look. Aside from lulls they hit over the Pacific and the Gulf of Mexico, they managed to race around the world in 20 days with no major crises, making a soft landing with their *Breitling Orbiter 3* balloon in the Egyptian desert. "When you are 30,000 feet in a balloon and you want to give up," said Piccard, 41, a psychiatrist, "you simply can't."

The team had a decisive edge. Their balloon, built at a cost of more than $3 million, featured an innovative layer of insulation around the gigantic helium chamber which reduced the gas's expansion and contraction, thus saving fuel needed to reheat it. And Jones, 52, a Royal Air Force veteran, has been a professional ballooning instructor for 10 years. As for Piccard, he had history on his side. His grandfather Auguste Piccard invented the pressurized gondola of modern ballooning and used it in 1931 to become the first person to reach the stratosphere.

"It was like a little piece of paradise," said Piccard (left, with Jones, and over the Swiss Alps).

After securing his place in the Cad Hall of Fame, Clinton toiled to make it up to his two women. Hillary's elective bid created a conflict between her roles as ambassador for the administration and as candidate needing to distance herself from it.

The Teflon Tandem

Clinton survives a Senate trial, while Hillary runs for her own seat there

As President Bill Clinton prepared for the impeachment trial resulting from his dalliance with a young White House intern, many Americans wondered if this would be the year that Hillary moved out. But when she announced her intention to relocate to a $1.7 million Dutch Colonial in a tony New York City suburb, it was for a different reason entirely: The Illinois native was just establishing residency in the state she aimed to represent in the U.S. Senate.

The President's 37-day trial, only the second in U.S. history, had capped a torturous yearlong public striptease of Clinton's private shenanigans, precipitated largely by his initial finger-wagging denial, "I did not have sexual relations with that woman, Ms. Lewinsky." When the hearing opened, the Senate took up the two articles of impeachment brought by the grim-faced House managers: perjury and obstruction of justice (in concealing his affair).

The Senate was tied, 50-50, on obstruction, less than the two-thirds required to convict.

BREAKING NEWS CNN LIVE
PRESIDENT CLINTON ACQUITTED OF BOTH IMPEACHMENT ARTICLES
12:44p ET

The carpetbagger candidate took heat for originally asking a Democrat fat cat to help finance their home (inset) and for professing to be a lifelong Yankee fan.

Charles Ruff, 59, the wheelchair-bound White House counsel, led the defense. Ending her Garbo-like silence, Monica Lewinsky, 26, was the star of the three witnesses, coming across (on her videotaped deposition) as candid and believable as she admitted to "mixed feelings" about the President and insisted that no one had asked her to lie. Clinton, 53, was less convincing when he pressed the refrain that he had been concentrating on the "people's business" rather than on his legal woes. After his acquittal, he told Americans he was "profoundly sorry . . . for what I said and did to trigger these events and the great burden they have imposed on the Congress and on the American people."

Everybody else tried to move on. Lewinsky appeared with Barbara Walters and published her story (with Princess Diana's collaborator Andrew Morton), in which she spoke swooningly of the President as an "incredible, sensual kisser." By year's end, she'd found love with a former *David Letterman* writer and a new career designing handbags.

First Daughter Chelsea, 19, continued at Stanford, keeping her college life private. Hillary, 52, who'd stood by her man through the trial, conjured a travel schedule that kept her out of Washington and in the headlines. As for the President, he was left alone to consider what life might await him as a senator's husband—and to contemplate his jumbled legacy.

In June, a poised Chelsea schmoozed with American GI's in Macedonia.

Cry, the Beloved Children

Serbia's furious campaign of ethnic cleansing turns Kosovo into a hell on earth

It seemed unthinkable. Little more than half a century after the Holocaust, which had given rise to the vow "never again," a genocidal fury was once more threatening Europe. This time the target area was the Balkans, the seeming madman was Yugoslav President Slobodan Milosevic, and the people in jeopardy were the ethnic Albanians of the tiny Serbian province of Kosovo. Through the winter months, Serb forces rounded up tens of thousands of men and boys of military age and killed some 10,000 of them. Another 1.2 million Kosovars were displaced from their homes, often at gunpoint. In the terror, some 35,000 women, children and elderly fled into Albania, Macedonia and Montenegro, a chaotic trail of tears that inadvertently separated 120,000 youths from their families. Survivors gave reports of water shortages and blackouts—and of seeing their fathers killed, their sisters raped, their homes burned.

On March 31, just one week after NATO initiated air strikes against Yugoslavia, the horror came home to Americans when three U.S. soldiers were captured by Serbian forces. For a month, they were pawns in the Balkan conflict before finally being released unharmed. By June, NATO peacekeeping troops had entered the province and Serb forces had exited, but the ethnic violence continued. "What's going on in the Balkans," declared Carol Bellamy, executive director of UNICEF, the U.N.'s children's relief agency, "is unmatched by anything in Europe since the aftermath of World War II."

At a refugee camp on the outskirts of Kukes, Albania, children raced toward French Puma helicopters delivering relief supplies.

A Lost Child Finds Her Family

At the Brazde camp in Macedonia, which provided temporary shelter for some 15,000 displaced Kosovars, Jehona Aliu, 5, drew a love letter for her parents and four siblings. She had lost track of her family at the Macedonian border after she stepped behind a tree to go to the bathroom. Miraculously, two weeks later she sat in her father Sadia's lap as the family were reunited in their ransacked Kosovo home (below).

A Mother Gets a New Start

Remzije Berisha, 29, tried to comfort 17-month-old Fjolla (left) while nursing her infant, who was born in the squalid Brazde camp. Because of the newborn, the Berishas were evacuated to better facilities in Germany (below). The child was christened Lejdina, Kosovar for "field," to mark the locale of her birth.

Life Becomes a Victory Lap

Five consummate competitors of the sports world hang it up in their 30s

JOHN ELWAY

His battered frame couldn't take it anymore. After 16 NFL seasons, back-to-back Super Bowl championships and a record 559 sacks taken over 256 games, Denver Broncos quarterback John Elway, 38, said, So long. Worth about $100 million, he plans to get some physical repairs done, make time for wife Janet and their children (below) "and enjoy life a little bit."

MICHAEL JORDAN

The world's most famous American finally opted for golf. Winner of six world championships with the Chicago Bulls and 10 scoring titles, earning at his peak $34 million a year, Michael Jordan, 36, walked away from basketball with his customary confidence and grace.

WAYNE GRETZKY

They called him the Great One. At 38, Wayne Gretzky could look back over 20 NHL seasons in which he ruled the sport. He'd missed being with wife Janet and their three kids, he explained, and had lost his mental edge.

STEFFI GRAF

"I'm not having fun anymore," said German-born tennis star Steffi Graf, 30. A pro by 13, she spent a record 377 weeks as the world's top-ranked woman. Planning to nurture her marketing company and mentor some younger tennis talent, Graf brought the fun back into her life by dating Andre Agassi, recently divorced from Brooke Shields.

JULIE KRONE

After 18 years in the saddle, winning more than 3,000 races, including the Belmont Stakes (the only woman to do so), and purses totaling some $80 million, jockey Julie Krone announced her decision to retire. "I'm on top," she said, "I'm 35, and I don't want to do this anymore."

Change in Tempo

Singer Celine Dion put her performing life aside in order to help her husband cope with cancer

Between her nonstop concert schedule and shopping for designer outfits (she owns 500 pairs of shoes), pop diva Celine Dion was planning to start a family with her husband and manager, René Angélil. Then in April doctors found, and removed, a cancerous growth on Angélil's neck, and Dion, 31, ducked out of a world tour to be with him. "René is the biggest priority in my life," she said, "and I want to be by his side as he continues his treatment." Just days after the surgery, Angélil, 57, was strong enough to play golf as he readied himself for six weeks of radiation therapy. And Dion went back on the road the end of May. The couple, who wed in 1994, are still hoping to conceive a child in the coming year. "From a medical standpoint," says Dr. Kathleen Behr, an assistant clinical professor of dermatology at UCLA, "having children is not a problem for patients with similar illnesses." Dion had already planned to take a year off after her tour-ending New Year's Eve millennium concert in Montreal. The youngest of 14 siblings, she's sure it's her time to be a mom, and quotes her doctor as saying, "You need to fly a little less, be home a little more. Just have a normal life, and the baby may want to be a part of it."

Call It the Tour de Lance

Armstrong's triumph in the greatest bike race capped his conquest of the disease

When Lance Armstrong, 27, finished the Tour de France (right) seven minutes ahead of his closest challenger, he became only the second American, after three-time champ Greg LeMond, to win the Super Bowl of cycling. To do it, Armstrong battled 180 of the toughest cyclists in the world, not to mention a torturous, 21-day, 2,287-mile course. But the Plano, Texas, native fought an even greater battle just to get to the starting line. For several months in 1996, Armstrong attributed the discomfort in his groin to bike-saddle soreness—until he began to cough and spit up blood. Diagnosed with advanced testicular cancer which had spread to his lungs, abdomen and brain, Armstrong was given survival odds of only 40 percent and even less chance of returning to the circuit.

Responding with the heart of a champion, he first studied his opponent. "I definitely did my homework," he said, before undergoing four rounds of chemo-

Armstrong and wife Kristin admire baby Luke.

therapy, an operation to remove lesions on his brain and another to remove a testicle. By early 1997 the cancer was gone, and doctors now say there's only a 2 percent chance of recurrence. One of his doctors, Jim Reeves, describes his recovery as "absolutely miraculous." To Armstrong, the case "sends a message that cancer is not a death sentence." And to that end, he has established a foundation dedicated to cancer awareness, and made frequent visits to children with the disease, whom he tells, "Cancer is the best thing that ever happened to me."

Well, maybe it's the second best. Three months after he took home the Tour victor's celebrated yellow jersey, his wife, Kristin, gave birth to their first child, Luke, who was conceived in vitro with sperm Armstrong had banked before starting chemotherapy. Dad now has homes in Austin, Texas, and Nice, France, a $400,000 book contract and a movie in the works.

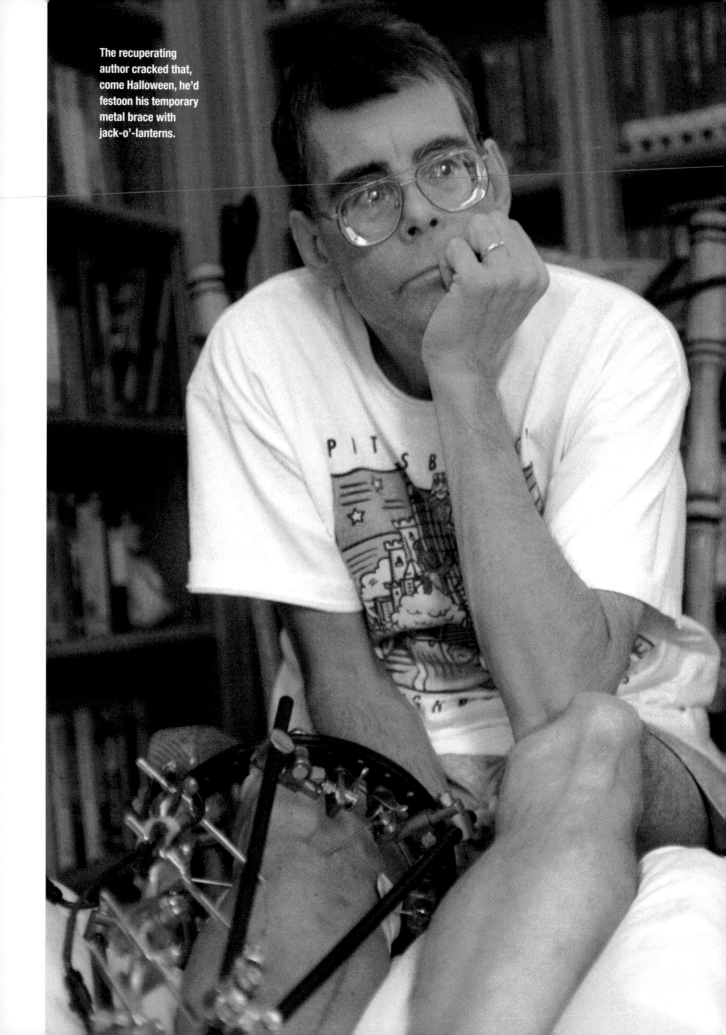

The recuperating author cracked that, come Halloween, he'd festoon his temporary metal brace with jack-o'-lanterns.

An Eerie Tale of Roadkill

Stephen King survives and caps a nightmare in his own inimitably grisly style

His neighbors mused about how the saga resembled *Misery,* his gruesome tale of a writer injured in a car accident, only to be tended—and tortured—by a demented nurse. But this wasn't Stephen King fiction, it was real, and the victim the horrormeister himself. While strolling one day near his Maine summer home, King, 51, was struck by a mini-van. The driver, Bryan Smith (who had been distracted by his passenger, a rottweiler named Pistol), thought from the crunch that he'd hit a deer. Rushed to Central Maine Medical Center in Lewiston, King underwent five separate surgeries aimed at stabilizing a collapsed lung and treating multiple fractures to his right leg and hip. He proved an amiable patient—getting updates on the Red Sox from his wife, Tabitha, and chuckling at jokes that his nurse was Kathy Bates (the creepy caregiver in the film *Misery*). But after his release, King complained of unprecedented writer's block, though he did retain his knack for the macabre ending, purchasing the van that hit him for $1,500. His plans? "I'm going to take a sledgehammer and beat the hell out of it."

Witness Chip Baker "was amazed he was alive."

Doctor Feel-Happy

The film smash based on Patch Adams's life won fans for a madcap medico but didn't quiet his critics

The real-life Dr. Patch Adams has a deep fondness for rubber noses and goofy hats, just like his zany doppelgänger played in the hit movie by Robin Williams. "I am a clown who is a doctor," says Adams, 53, whose use of rowdy humor has made him both famous and controversial in the field. But unlike the celluloid hero, Adams doesn't currently have either a hospital or patients. Back in 1980, he did acquire a 310-acre site for his nonprofit Gesundheit! Institute in Pocahontas County, West Virginia. And then, three years later, he gave up the practice that made his name—treating patients at free clinics in that state and Virginia—to begin fund-raising for the facility. But so far Adams has accumulated only $1 million of the $26 million required to build his theme-park-like hospital, in which, for example, the eye clinic will be shaped like an eyeball. Critics of the grandiose plan include Linda Edquist, his wife for 23 years (they went through a painful divorce in 1998) and mother of their sons, Atomic Zagnut and Lars Zig. "I would have settled for a much smaller place," she says, adding that her ex is "not the same person he was 15 years ago. If you're constantly told how wonderful you are, you start to believe it." Still, supporters of Adams's crusade for compassionate doctoring remain loyal. Says Rick Wade, senior VP of the American Hospital Association (which represents health care organizations): "Most doctors won't ever achieve what Patch is talking about. But it's a hell of a thing to motivate you in the morning."

Olympian Quest

Zing went the strings of her new bow, as
Geena Davis sought stardom in a fresh field

What do you do if you're an Oscar winner but aging in Hollywood-leading-lady years (43) and looking for something to do "besides reading scripts all day"? For Geena Davis, the unlikely answer was archery. Her inspiration came from fellow Californian Justin Huish, 21, who had dramatically won two golds in the 1996 Olympics. Within months, Davis was training with Huish's coach Don Rabska. Her not-so-modest goal: to represent the U.S. at the 2000 Olympics in Sydney. "Geena is very focused," marveled Rabska, as his star student practiced five hours a day, six days a week and even on the soundstage during her filming of *Stuart Little*. "Archery is a battle with yourself," Davis said. "It's really addictive." She did come "very far," cheered Huish, "smoking people who have been at it 10 years." But at the August trials to pick the four-member U.S. squad, Davis finished 24th of 28. "At my advanced age, to be able to do something athletic and excel is very meaningful," concluded the twice-divorced Davis. But, she added, "I have to keep making movies."

Her Fave Color Is Green

Martha Stewart makes a
gaffe in Washington—and
a killing on Wall Street

It was a year in which Our Lady of Domestic Perfection fared better in the trading pits of Wall Street than in the President's parlor. In June, Martha Stewart rattled teacups by showing up at a White House soiree for the president of Hungary in pink cropped pants. "I admire Martha Stewart tremendously," says Letitia Baldrige, social secretary during the Kennedy years. "But I think she needs to read other people's books on how to dress properly for such an occasion. A state dinner means a long dress to the floor." Responded the House of Stewart: "Martha felt it was appropriate, and she said a number of people complimented her on it."

And Stewart's real stock was hardly diminished. In October she stage-managed a tasteful initial public offering that evaluated her empire at $873.2 million—and that was before the 7.2 million shares had even hit the Big Board. On the morning that Martha Stewart Living Omnimedia debuted, a conservatively dressed Stewart circulated on the floor of the New York Stock Exchange while the shares gained a tidy 100 percent in a single day for investors lucky enough to be in on the NYSE's hottest IPO in years. Stewart herself was worth more than $600 million on paper *prior* to the opening. But the shelf life of the First Name in Gracious Living may not be forever. She is 58, and *The New York Times,* in a show of lèse-majesté, compared Stewart Inc. to Minnie Pearl's Fried Chicken.

A Very Happenin' Buddhist

The Dalai Lama's mission to America draws crowds and creates two bestsellers

With his bald pate and soft-spoken manner, he seems an unlikely celebrity. But the Dalai Lama, 64, the 14th heir to Tibet's 600-year-old religious dynasty, attracted a crowd of more than 40,000 people to New York City's Central Park in August for a summer lecture on tolerance and nonviolence. Introduced by actor Richard Gere (below, right), whose foundation helped bankroll the Dalai Lama's four-day visit, the Buddhist leader spoke for more than an hour. Alluding to his life in exile since age 24, following China's takeover of his Himalayan country, he intoned, "My life, when I look back, has not been easy. But one thing I learned: The compassion, the sense of caring about others' welfare, brings to me inner strength." The tour was just one indication of the Dalai Lama's remarkable worldwide popularity. Two of his books, *The Art of Happiness* and *Ethics for the New Millennium,* climbed onto the *New York Times'* bestseller list—then stayed and stayed.

The Dalai Lama's August teach-in marked his second visit to Central Park. In 1991, the Nobel Peace Prize winner had attracted only 5,000.

"I feel as if our country were reborn," says Leah Rabin of Barak (right, at a political rally in May).

Battling for Peace

Ex-commando and new prime minister Ehud Barak aims to pave Israel's path toward a lasting settlement with the Palestinians

While growing up on Kibbutz Mishmar HaSharon, north of Tel Aviv, Ehud Barak got a reputation as a Houdini who could pick any lock. With his landslide May victory over hard-line prime minister Benjamin Netanyahu, Barak, 57, now must pull off his deftest feat yet: healing the Jewish state's religious and political rifts and getting peace negotiations with the Palestinians back on track. With his election, Barak—the Hebrew word for lightning—stirred excitement beyond the country's borders. Jordan's King Abdullah predicted "a new phase of peace and stability in the region." And in November, Barak and Palestinian leader Yasir Arafat pledged to hold regular meetings, in hopes of hammering out a truce framework by February.

Barak's military record hardly suggests a con-ciliator. When Palestinian terrorists hijacked an airliner in 1972, he led a team that stormed the jet and saved all but one of the 99 passengers. A year later, disguised as a woman, Barak hunted down terrorists involved with the PLO attack that killed 11 Israeli athletes at the Munich Olympics. In 1976 he helped orchestrate the Entebbe raid from Nairobi, Kenya. The eldest of four sons, Barak dropped out of high school, then, while in the army, earned degrees from Jerusalem's Hebrew University. It was there that he met his wife, Nava, 50, with whom he has three daughters. In 1995 he was tapped by then prime minister Yitzhak Rabin to be interior minister. "Only people who have seen the ugly face of war," says Rabin's widow, Leah, "are there to fight the hardest for peace."

Plato (in 1998) "had a very engaging spirit," says *Diff'rent Strokes* costar Conrad Bain.

Strokes of Bad Luck

Lovable child star Dana Plato grew up to be an addict, an alcoholic and, with her death, a Hollywood casualty

At her memorial service, friends remembered Dana Plato, 34, as an overgrown little girl who loved butterflies, rainbows and sunsets. But by the time she was 15, with 250 commercials already to her credit and a starring role in the popular NBC sitcom *Diff'rent Strokes,* Plato had developed a taste for far more dangerous substances: alcohol and prescription drugs. When Plato, who publicly admitted to Valium and alcohol abuse, swallowed lethal doses of the pain relievers Soma and Lortab in May, many friends believed it was an accident; police, however, ruled it a suicide.

Either way, her tragic ending in a Winnebago in Moore, Oklahoma, reflected the quagmire of drugs and scandal that Plato's life had become. At 18 she was written out of *Diff'rent Strokes* after becoming pregnant. An adopted child herself whose parents had divorced before she was 4, Plato had a rough time being a mother to her son Tyler, now 14, who was mostly raised by his father (Lanny Lambert, from whom Plato had parted in 1989) and paternal grandmother. Plato crossed the line from fame to notoriety in 1991, when she donned dark glasses to hold up a Las Vegas video store with a pellet gun, making off with $164. It took a stranger, singer Wayne Newton, to post her $13,000 bail.

Though Plato once earned $25,000 an episode for her series, she was often broke. In 1989 she posed for *Playboy*; the following year she worked as a cashier in a Las Vegas dry-cleaning shop. By the time she hit her nadir, starring in a '97 soft-core porn flick, Plato had become that tragic cliché of the TV age: the cute child star who stumbles into adulthood—then free-falls.

Down, Out and Looking for a Break

"I'm not dead yet; I haven't retired. But I have four strikes against me," maintained *Diff'rent Strokes* star Gary Coleman, 31. "I'm black, I'm short, I'm intelligent and I have a medical condition." In August, Coleman, who at 10 commanded $70,000 an episode, admitted to a fifth strike: He was broke. His announcement, just four months after Plato's death, reminded America that the *Strokes* kids have endured brutal growing pains. (The third young member of the cast, Todd Bridges, 33, developed a cocaine habit and a police record.) When he declared his bankruptcy in L.A. (above), Coleman, who suffers from end-stage renal disease, insisted this was a chance to start over. "Millions do it," he said.

After their days on the set (with Charlotte Rae and Bain in '79), Todd Bridges (left), Coleman (center) and Plato ran into trouble.

A Real General's Daughter

Courageous Nancy Mace prevails as The Citadel's first female graduate

Professors called her Mr. Mace. Classmates shunned her. And one upperclassman memorably "stared a hole through my head," recalls Nancy Mace, 21, of her early days at The Citadel. But in May, when Mace became the first woman to graduate from the 156-year-old South Carolina military institution, that hostile upperclassman, now a divinity student, came back to watch. "She won him over," says her mother. "As she did many others, because of who she is and her absolute commitment to do well."

Mace excelled from the start, beating 145 out of 150 cadets in a two-mile run and polishing off 59 push-ups in two minutes (making her one of only four freshmen to pass that first fitness test). By the time she graduated, magna cum laude, this gutsy Army brat (her father, a retired general, is The Citadel's most decorated living graduate) was hailed by school president John Grinalds as "not only a pioneer but a pacesetter for those who will follow her."

Many will. The school now has 41 female cadets, and the total could rise to 100 next year. That's a dramatic change since 1995, when The Citadel was forced by court order to go coed, and Shannon Faulkner became the first, only to drop out after six harrowing days. Mace is modest about her role. "You see positive leadership and negative leadership," she says. "You take the positive." In that spirit, she became engaged to classmate Chris Niemiec, 21, and took a prestigious training position with Andersen Consulting.

Queen of Peace

Surprising doubters—and herself—Rana Raslan becomes the first Arab to be named Miss Israel

An olive-skinned Mediterranean stunner with a radiant smile, Rana Raslan had always enjoyed posing for the camera. So it should not have seemed surprising that among the 20 young women (winnowed from a field of 800) to compete in the Miss Israel contest in March, Raslan captured the crown. What made her victory a shocker was that the Jewish state's new reigning beauty isn't Jewish—she's an Arab. "I want to say something," Raslan, 22, told the audience that night. "I will represent Israel in the best manner possible. It doesn't matter if I am an Arab or a Jew. We must show the world that we can live together." Raised in the Islamic faith, Raslan has known difficult times. Her parents, an electrician and a hotel cook, divorced when she was 13; two years later a brother was imprisoned for assault. A beauty contestant since age 15, Raslan heeded her mother's caution not to expect too much, "because they always pick Jews, not Arabs." Now Raslan commands higher modeling fees and hopes to see the world.

"This isn't politics," says Raslan (above, with a street vendor). "This is a beauty contest."

An Antipodal Adventure Tale

Dr. Jerri Nielsen, a medical heroine, gives chemotherapy to herself

"It has been a Hell of an adventure but not the one that I had planned," Dr. Jerri Nielsen e-mailed friends, just a couple of months before a Hercules cargo plane was finally able to swoop down through the brutal Antarctic weather and lift her off the polar icecap; the operation was completed in 22 minutes lest the plane's hydraulic fluids freeze. An ER physician from Canfield, Ohio, Nielsen, 47, took over the hospital at the Amundsen-Scott research station after a divorce that left her husband, Jay, with custody of their three children. She adored the desolate beauty of "my beloved Antarctic Plateau" and the camaraderie of her 40 colleagues, but in June she notified HQ back home that she had found a lump in her breast. Midwinter temperatures of 80 below precluded an evacuation, so diagnostic equipment and anticancer drugs were air-dropped in, along with fresh fruit and vegetables for all. A few days later, the redoubtable Nielsen gave herself a local anesthetic, inserted a needle into her breast, withdrew tissue for a biopsy and transmitted digital images of the tumor cells over the Internet. For the next three months Nielsen administered her own chemo, then, upon her return to the States, underwent surgery, and released an upbeat statement that concluded, "My spirit is strong."

Wildly Off Course

Taken at the top of his game, stylish golfer
Payne Stewart dies in a baffling plane crash

It was shaping up to be a banner year for golfer Payne Stewart. Not
only had the champ, famed for his retro knickers and tam-o'-shanters,
clinched his second U.S. Open title in June (this time with a dramatic
15-ft. putt on the final hole), but at 42 he was enjoying a newfound
serenity. His only complaint seemed to be that the 10-month PGA
Tour grind kept him away from his wife of 18 years, Tracey, 42, and
their two kids, Chelsea, 13, and Aaron, 10. In an effort to carve out
more family time, Stewart, like a number of pro golfers, traveled by
private jet. Thus, on October 25, Stewart chartered a Learjet 35 to
fly from his home city of Orlando to Dallas for the final PGA event
of the 1999 season. But less than 30 minutes into
the flight, the plane lost contact with air traffic
control, then veered off course on an eerie, appar-
ently autopilot journey of some 1,400 miles, before
running out of fuel and plummeting into a field
in South Dakota. Tragically, Stewart and the five
others on board were killed.

**Stewart shares his
June U.S. Open
triumph with wife
Tracey, and got jiggy
after a 1991 victory
in Minnesota.**

PARTY ANIMALS

OSCARS

Gwyneth Paltrow was in the pink.

Every year, the show world's best and buffest convene to honor their achievements and preen for the camera. At home, we're guaranteed laughter (not always intentional), tears (especially from the winners), acres of sleek flesh and the pick of the couture litter.

Best Actor **ROBERTO BENIGNI**'s speeches could've used subtitles; his exuberance needed none. He levitated when his *Life Is Beautiful* got Best Foreign Oscar.

The Oscars

71ST ANNUAL ACADEMY AWARDS

(Presented March 22, 1999)
Picture: *Shakespeare in Love* Actor:
Roberto Benigni, *Life Is Beautiful* Actress:
Gwyneth Paltrow, *Shakespeare in Love*
Supporting Actor: James Coburn,
Affliction Supporting Actress: Judi
Dench, *Shakespeare in Love* Director:
Steven Spielberg, *Saving Private Ryan*
Original Screenplay: Mark Norman
and Tom Stoppard, *Shakespeare in
Love* Adapted Screenplay:
Bill Condon, *Gods and Monsters*
Original Song: Stephen
Schwartz, "When You Believe,"
from *The Prince of Egypt*
Honorary Award: Elia
Kazan Cinematography:
Janusz Kaminski, *Saving Private
Ryan* Original Musical or
Comedy Score: Stephen War-
beck, *Shakespeare in Love* Origi-
nal Dramatic Score: Nicola
Piovani, *Life Is Beautiful*
Documentary: James
Moll and Ken Lipper,
The Last Days

Welsh beauty
**CATHERINE ZETA-
JONES** called her Ver-
sace "an event dress."

At *Vanity Fair*'s
Oscar bash, **DAISY
FUENTES** listens
while **JIM CARREY**
riffs, and **PAMELA
ANDERSON LEE**
thinks whatever **TIM
ALLEN** just said is a
classical gas.

Oh, behave! *Austin
Powers* creator and star
MIKE MYERS pre-
sented the award for best
makeup and got cheeky
with wife **ROBIN** at the
Miramax party.

Hostess **WHOOPI
GOLDBERG**
didn't just talk funny,
she dressed funny, in
outfits that spoofed the
year's films.

In her fedora and back-to-front pants suit, both by Christian Dior, chanteuse **CELINE DION** deserved an award for eccentricity —and nerve. (Yes, that is the way the jacket's worn.)

Sweet young thing on the rise **LIV TYLER** gets a kiss from Dad, Aerosmith's ageless bad boy **STEVEN**. Even at the Oscars, there's a place for family values.

CATE BLANCHETT, up for *Elizabeth* (and in Vera Wang), "put on a Madonna CD and danced around" to get in the party mood.

Golden Globes

56TH ANNUAL GOLDEN GLOBE AWARDS

(Presented January 24, 1999)

MOTION PICTURES Drama: *Saving Private Ryan* Actor, Drama: Jim Carrey, *The Truman Show* Actress, Drama: Cate Blanchett, *Elizabeth* Musical or Comedy: *Shakespeare in Love* Actor, Musical or Comedy: Michael Caine, *Little Voice* Actress, Musical or Comedy: Gwyneth Paltrow, *Shakespeare in Love* Supporting Actor: Ed Harris, *The Truman Show* Supporting Actress: Lynn Redgrave, *Gods & Monsters* Director: Steven Spielberg, *Saving Private Ryan* Screenplay: Mark Norman and Tom Stoppard, *Shakespeare in Love*

TELEVISION Drama Series: *The Practice* Actor, Drama Series: Dylan McDermott, *The Practice* Actress, Drama Series: Keri Russell, *Felicity* Musical or Comedy Series: *Ally McBeal* Actor, Musical or Comedy Series: Michael J. Fox, *Spin City* Actress, Musical or Comedy Series: Jenna Elfman, *Dharma & Greg*

SHARON STONE and hubby **PHIL BRONSTEIN** clinched without crushing her Vera Wang.

Felicity's **KERI RUSSELL** looked every inch the winner in her "fancy hippie-chick" Armani.

GOLDEN GLOBES

Smart in a beaded Armani, **JODIE FOSTER** planned to be back home with baby Charles by 10 p.m.

Pals **CAMERON DIAZ** and **GWYNETH PALTROW** had a major hair thing going.

JACK NICHOLSON got a Lifetime Achievement Award and a smooch from **WARREN BEATTY.**

The Emmys

51ST ANNUAL EMMY AWARDS

(Presented September 12, 1999)
Drama Series: *The Practice* Comedy Series: *Ally McBeal* Variety, Music or Comedy Series: *Late Show with David Letterman* Miniseries: *Horatio Hornblower* Lead Actor, Drama Series: Dennis Franz, *N.Y.P.D. Blue* Lead Actress, Drama Series: Edie Falco, *The Sopranos* Lead Actor, Comedy Series: John Lithgow, *Third Rock from the Sun* Lead Actress, Comedy Series: Helen Hunt, *Mad About You* Lead Actor, Miniseries or Special: Stanley Tucci, *Winchell* Lead Actress, Miniseries or Special: Helen Mirren, *The Passion of Ayn Rand* Supporting Actor, Drama: Michael Badalucco, *The Practice* Supporting Actress, Drama: Holland Taylor, *The Practice* Supporting Actor, Miniseries or Special: Peter O'Toole, *Joan of Arc* Supporting Actress, Miniseries or Special: Anne Bancroft, *Deep in My Heart*

The buzz about a purported bout with anorexia is past, and **CALISTA FLOCKHART** stood sleek and stylish in a Ralph Lauren ensemble.

They went home with no Emmys, but **BRAD PITT** and **JENNIFER ANISTON** (in Randolph Duke) look awfully pleased with their consolation prizes: each other.

3rd Rock's **KRISTEN JOHNSTON** (a Supporting Actress winner) and **DEBRA MESSING** (of *Will & Grace*) share a hug as well as a dress designer: Randolph Duke.

Vampire Slayer **SARAH MICHELLE GELLAR** looked to die for in her slinky backless Vera Wang. A presenter this year, she pronounced the whole shindig "pretty smooth."

Who looks prouder, *The Practice*'s elegantly tuxed **STEVE HARRIS** or his spiffy mom, **MATTIE**?

DAVID E. KELLEY celebrated his double win with a snuggle with his main squeeze, Armani-clad **MICHELLE PFEIFFER**.

61

On her 19th Best Actress nomination in the Daytime Emmys, **SUSAN LUCCI** finally scored. Lucci, 52, had played the soap world's most infamous devil woman, *All My Children*'s Erica Kane (above), since 1969, and her losing streak had become a joke everywhere except in her Garden City, New York, household. The quintessential suburbanite in real life, Lucci dotes on her family (in 1990, below), which includes her manager husband of 30 years, Helmut Huber, and two kids. Daughter Liza is on rival soap *Passions*.

The Daytime Emmys

26TH ANNUAL DAYTIME EMMY AWARDS

(Presented May 22, 1999)
Drama: *General Hospital* Talk Show: *The Rosie O'Donnell Show* Game Show: *Win Ben Stein's Money* Actor: **Anthony Geary**, *General Hospital* Actress: **Susan Lucci**, *All My Children* Supporting Actor: **Stuart Damon**, *General Hospital* Supporting Actress: **Sharon Case**, *The Young and the Restless* Talk Show Host: **Rosie O'Donnell** Lifetime Achievement Award: **Bob Barker**

No snob, *Gia* star **ANGELINA JOLIE** confessed to having stopped by McDonald's before the ceremony.

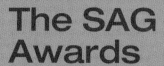

ER's **ALEX KINGSTON** said of Brits (like **BEN KINGSLEY**): We party all night and happily "come to the set looking like dogs."

The SAG Awards

5TH ANNUAL SCREEN ACTORS GUILD AWARDS

(Presented March 7, 1999)

FILM Actor: Roberto Benigni, *Life Is Beautiful*. Actress: Gwyneth Paltrow, *Shakespeare in Love* Supporting Actor: Robert Duvall, *A Civil Action* Supporting Actress: Kathy Bates, *Primary Colors* Motion Picture Cast: *Shakespeare in Love*

TELEVISION Actor, Movie or Miniseries: Christopher Reeve, *Rear Window* Actress, Movie or Miniseries: Angelina Jolie, *Gia* Actor, Drama Series: Sam Waterson, *Law & Order* Actress, Drama Series: Julianna Margulies, *ER* Actor, Comedy Series: Michael J. Fox, *Spin City* Actress, Comedy Series: Tracey Ullman, *Tracy Takes On…* Ensemble, Drama Series: *ER* Ensemble, Comedy Series: *Ally McBeal* Lifetime Achievement Award: Kirk Douglas

Friends of a (black) feather **LISA KUDROW, COURTENEY COX** and **JENNIFER ANISTON** flocked together. Cox assured the world that her rubberized Dolce & Gabbana was actually very comfortable.

Fans literally screamed for **KIRK DOUGLAS**, here with another legend, **LAUREN BACALL**, who was a presenter.

LAURYN HILL won an unprecedented (for a female artist) five Grammys and rejoiced by reading the 40th Psalm aloud onstage.

"It was worth the wait," said the kimono-clad **MADONNA**, who in her 16 years had taken home only a video Grammy.

The Grammys

41ST ANNUAL GRAMMY AWARDS

(Presented February 24, 1999)

Record of the Year: *My Heart Will Go On*, Celine Dion Song of the Year: "My Heart Will Go On," Celine Dion Album of the Year: *The Miseducation of Lauryn Hill*, Lauryn Hill New Artist: Lauryn Hill Male Pop Vocal: "My Father's Eyes," Eric Clapton Female Pop Vocal: "My Heart Will Go On," Celine Dion Pop Vocal by a Duo or Group: "Jump Jive an' Wail," Brian Setzer Orchestra Pop Album: *Ray of Light*, Madonna Rock Song: "Uninvited," Alanis Morissette Male Rock Vocal: "Fly Away," Lenny Kravitz Female Rock Vocal: "Uninvited," Alanis Morissette Rock Vocal by a Duo or Group: "Pink," Aerosmith R&B Song: "Doo Wop (That Thing)," Lauryn Hill Rap Solo: "Gettin' Jiggy Wit It," Will Smith

BRANDY & MONICA arrived at the event holding hands and sang a duet, determined to show that rumors of a feud were just that.

GRAMMYS

A newly svelte **VINCE GILL** (in Dolce & Gabbana) sang with Hall of Fame inductee **DOLLY PARTON.**

The CMAs

53RD ANNUAL COUNTRY MUSIC AWARDS

(Presented September 22, 1999)

Entertainer: **Shania Twain** Male Vocalist: **Tim McGraw** Female Vocalist: **Martina McBride** Single: **"Wide Open Spaces,"** Dixie Chicks Album: *A Place in the Sun,* **Tim McGraw** Vocal Group: **Dixie Chicks** Vocal Duo: **Brooks & Dunn** Music Video: **"Wide Open Spaces,"** Dixie Chicks Horizon Award: **Jo Dee Messina** Song: **"This Kiss,"** Annie Roboff, **Robin Lerner, Beth Nielsen Chapman** Event: **Vince Gill and Patty Loveless,** *My Kind of Woman/My Kind of Man*

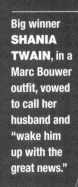

Big winner **SHANIA TWAIN,** in a Marc Bouwer outfit, vowed to call her husband and "wake him up with the great news."

TIM McGRAW said he and wife **FAITH HILL** planned to celebrate "with steak and eggs at home."

"It doesn't matter how uncomfortable you are as long as you look good," said **BROOKE SHIELDS**, vamping in Versace.

People's Choice Awards

25TH ANNUAL PEOPLE'S CHOICE AWARDS

(Presented January 10, 1999)

TELEVISION Male Performer: Tim Allen Female Performer: Helen Hunt Male, New Series: Nathan Lane, *Encore! Encore!* Female, New Series: Christina Applegate, *Jesse* New Comedy Series: *Jesse* and *Will & Grace* (Tie) New Dramatic Series: *L.A. Doctors* Dramatic Series: *ER* Comedy Series: *Seinfeld* and *Frasier* (Tie) Male Musical Performer: Garth Brooks Female Musical Performer: Celine Dion FILM Actor: **Tom Hanks** Actress: **Sandra Bullock** Comedy: *There's Something About Mary* Drama: *Titanic* All-Time Favorite Motion Picture Performer: **Harrison Ford** All-Time Favorite Television Performer: **Bill Cosby** All-Time Favorite Musical Performer: **Elton John**

Eat before the show was the advice of **SANDRA BULLOCK**. Her Badgley Mischka didn't show it.

Of his latest award, **KELSEY GRAMMER** (with wife **CAMILLE**) said modestly, "I don't have that many. I have a few."

A galaxy of movie favorites—**JUDI DENCH, MARTIN SHORT, BERNADETTE PETERS** and **BRIAN DENNEHEY**—glowed as moonlighters on the stage.

The Tonys

53RD ANNUAL TONY AWARDS

(Presented June 6, 1999)

Play: *Side Man*, Warren Leight Musical: *Fosse*
Actor, Play: Brian Dennehy, *Death of a Salesman*
Actress, Play: Dame Judi Dench, *Amy's View*
Actor, Musical: Martin Short, *Little Me* Actress,
Musical: Bernadette Peters, *Annie Get Your Gun*
Choreography: Matthew Bourne, *Swan Lake*
Revival, Play: *Death of a Salesman* Revival,
Musical: *Annie Get your Gun*

MTV Movie Awards

53RD ANNUAL MTV MOVIE AWARDS

(Presented June 5, 1999)

Film: *There's Something About Mary* Actor:
Jim Carrey, *The Truman Show* Actress:
Cameron Diaz, *There's Something About
Mary* Best Comedic Performance:
Ben Stiller, *The Waterboy* Best Break-
through Performances: James
Van Der Beek, *Varsity Blues*, and
Katie Holmes, *Disturbing Behavior*
Best Villain: Matt Dillon, *There's
Something About Mary*, and
Stephen Dorff, *Blade* (Tie)
Best Kiss: Gwyneth Paltrow
and Joseph Fiennes,
Shakespeare in Love

At first he went unrec-
ognized in his hippie
threads, an outfit that
suggested **JIM
CARREY** might be
just stopping by en
route to a Grateful
Dead concert.

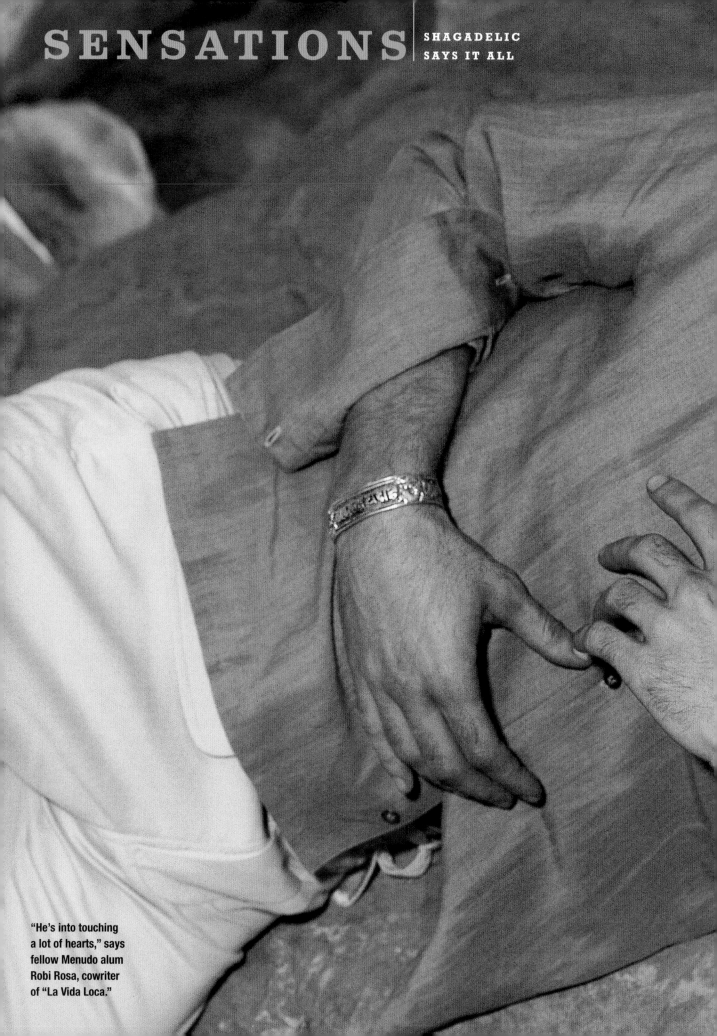

"He's into touching
a lot of hearts," says
fellow Menudo alum
Robi Rosa, cowriter
of "La Vida Loca."

Lovin'
Livin' la
Vida Loca

Maybe it's Latin heat wave
Ricky Martin who's really to
blame for global warming.

He'd been a Menudo at 12, toiled a year on a soap and starred on Broadway in *Les Misérables,* so no one could say that he hadn't paid his dues before February's Grammycast. That was the night his ebullient grin and killer swivel seduced a worldwide audience exceeding a billion, and suddenly, at 27, Ricky Martin was enthroned as global entertainment's enchilada-in-chief. In the mop-up that followed, his salsa single "Livin' la Vida Loca" became the hit of the summer, and his five albums passed the 18 million sales mark. He recorded a duet with Madonna and performed benefits with Sting and Luciano Pavarotti. An icon to fellow Latinos now had a whole galaxy of teens squealing after him in hordes, and their moms didn't mind. Says Lilly Melgar, a castmate on *General Hospital*: "People just love and adore Ricky. He has a regal presence with the spirit of a child."

A onetime altar boy from Puerto Rico, he was the only child of an accountant, Nereida Morales, and a psychologist, Enrique Martin III. He had shot 11 commercials (including Burger King and Orange Crush) by the time he became the youngest Menudo on his second audition. (He flunked the first for being too short but now stands 6'2".) Five years later, Martin was basking in fame, money—and burnout. So in 1989 he quit the group and, exhausted by the nonstop touring and estranged from his parents, retreated to the Queens area of New York City, where he worked out, visited museums and regirded his loins. By 1992, he was back onstage and on TV in Mexico City, where he recorded his first album of original songs. *Ricky Martin* went platinum, and his 1993 follow-up disc won him a Billboard award for Best New Latin Artist. The same year, he moved to L.A. in hopes of launching a movie career and wound up in *General Hospital* as bartender Miquel Morez. He briefly dated Lili Melgar, who played his love on the soap, but, as he explained at the time, "right now I'm going out with someone who is very jealous. Her name is My Career. [For her] I give up everything."

Martin had long since reconciled with his mother, who

His *Today* appearance in June caused a presidential-visit-level traffic jam in New York City. Katie Couric called him "infectious."

had taken charge of his ample finances. And in 1995, with the death of his paternal grandfather (and some help from therapy), Martin decided to reach out to his dad. "One of us had to let go of the past and take the first step," figured Ricky. "He was the father. I knew it had to be me." Today the two talk at least once a week, though Ricky has settled in Miami. He did his five-bedroom, Mediterranean-style refuge mostly in white, says his decorator, Rene T. Rodriguez, to create a "Zen-like existence." "Success can be lethal," Martin told a San Juan magazine, and he calls himself a "very spiritual" person who's into Buddhism, yoga and meditation. "Silence is very important to me," he tapped out to fans, perhaps wishfully, in a recent online chat. So far, he's managed to keep his life relatively simple (except for a penchant for Armani clothes) and private, keeping quiet about his on-off relationship with Mexican TV personality Rebecca de Alba, 30. But Trudie Styler, a fan who got him to perform at her husband Sting's Rainforest concert, predicts that Martin is about to become "an Elvis-like phenomenon." Get ready for "Viva la Vida Vegas."

The Ricky craze has become Sinatraesque, if not Beatlemaniacal.

Just a Typical Teen Megastar

At 17, Britney Spears moved from playing the mall to becoming a major minor

Less than a year earlier, Britney Spears was belting out her bubblegum ditties in shopping malls and loving every minute of it. "No one knew who I was, but I could see they really enjoyed the music. And," she adds, "I got *a lot* of shopping done." Then Spears's album, *...Baby One More Time,* and its title single entered the charts at No. 1 in the same week, a first for a debut solo act. It all seemed preordained for a kid who'd performed for imaginary audiences at age 2 in Kentwood, Louisiana. By 11, she was making commercials in New York City before landing a part on *The Mickey Mouse Club,* working alongside such future stars as Keri Russell (of TV's *Felicity*) and members of 'N Sync. When Spears turned 15, her mother sent out a demo tape. Two years later, she is a certified teen queen, and constant touring interferes with her home schooling and social life. But you'll hear no complaints from Spears. "It's so awesome just to hear your song on the radio and see your video on MTV! This is unreal!" she shouts, sounding remarkably like the wannabes who throng her performances.

Goofing around on a rare visit home, Spears stomps her big bro Bryan, 21.

Giving Soccer a Kick

The U.S. women win the World Cup and inspire girls across America

Forget the Spice Girls. The Nice Girls, a genuinely clean-cut and absolutely charming collection of 20 world-class soccer players, emerged as the pop culture heroines of the year. In a gripping match against China decided in an overtime shootout, the U.S. soccer team claimed a 5-4 victory in the finals of the Women's World Cup. Their dazzling July performance drew a deafening crowd of 90,185 to the Rose Bowl in Pasadena, and about as many TV viewers (40 million) as the NBA finals.

But in an era when drug tests, DWIs and gazillion-dollar contracts are as much a part of the sports lexicon as slam dunks and double plays, the exuberant athletes touched a nerve with their grit, hustle, skill and passion for the game. "From day one," says Mia Hamm, 27, the team's scoring sensation, "we've played because we love to play."

It helps that the athletes offer a snapshot of the real world: a mix of ethnicities, of working moms and single gals. It doesn't hurt that Team Too Good to Be True is "Babe City," as avid fan David Letterman gushed on his show. For some viewers, the most memorable moment came when comely defender Brandi Chastain, 31, stripped off her jersey after scoring on her final penalty kick, which (thanks to goalie Briana Scurry's clutch save moments before) won the Cup for the Yanks. Now these role-model jocks can dream more realistically of a professional league of their own.

With her bodice-ripping finale, Chastain embodied the Team USA ebullience. (The slight white blur is the pattern of the net, through which the picture was taken.)

A Special Romeo for Julia

After a string of fizzled romances, Roberts gets cozy with Benjamin Bratt

Like clockwork, she homers with film after film: 1997's *My Best Friend's Wedding*, 1998's *Stepmom*, 1999's *Notting Hill* and *Runaway Bride*. And like clockwork, she strikes out with celeb after celeb: Dylan McDermott, Liam Neeson, ex-fiancé Kiefer Sutherland and ex-husband Lyle Lovett, to name a few. But since late 1997, Julia Roberts, 32, one of Hollywood's most canonized, criticized and scrutinized actresses, has been spotted all over the world arm in arm with just one hunk: Benjamin Bratt. Whether or not Bratt, 36, is a keeper, Roberts is plainly smitten with the dashing actor she calls simply "my man." "Julia is incredibly happy right now," says a close friend, adding, "The relationship is so special that none of us wants to comment."

Fans caught a glimpse of their magnetism last May when Roberts guest-starred on *Law & Order,* the hit NBC drama that made Bratt a star. The episode, which netted Roberts an Emmy nomination, was one of Bratt's last; at season's end, he quit the series to get more personal time. Like Roberts, Bratt is close to his mother (a Peruvian-born activist for Native Americans)—and is coping with a deep family rift. (Roberts is estranged from her actor brother Eric, 43; Bratt lost contact with his father when he was 25.) Perhaps because both stars come from broken families—both were 4 when their parents divorced—they have made each other top priority.

Runaway Bride was a runaway hit for Roberts (left, with costar Richard Gere), but the runaway event of her life is her relationship with Bratt (her date, above, at the film's L.A. premiere).

Mission Irrepressible

Mike Myers unleashes his alter egomaniac, Austin Powers, one more time

"Yeah, baby!" Superswinging Austin Powers returned for a sequel spoof of James Bond and the groovy '60s in *The Spy Who Shagged Me,* and raked in $55 million opening weekend. Almost equally rewarding for Austin's antic concocter, Mike Myers, 36, is getting a new verb—shag—into the next edition of the *Encarta World English Dictionary.* The nuttily inventive Canadian comic previously created the "farklemt" Linda Richman, a parody of his mother-in-law, for *Saturday Night Live,* as well as Wayne Campbell, the teenage heavy-metal freak and costar of the two *Wayne's World* flicks. In private, Myers is a bookworm and rabid Toronto Maple Leafs fan who watches war footage on TV while painting toy soldiers. He got his start shoot-ing commercials at 4 and later joined the Second City troupe, and he credits the film characters he conceived—not just Powers but also the dread Dr. Evil and the flatulent spy Fat Bastard—to the British humor of his late father, an encyclopedia salesman from Liverpool. His present muse is his wife of six years, actress-writer Robin Ruzan, 35, who, fed up with his using his "Do I make you horny?" shtick around their Hollywood Hills home, snapped, "Why don't you just write a movie?"

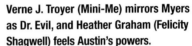

Verne J. Troyer (Mini-Me) mirrors Myers as Dr. Evil, and Heather Graham (Felicity Shagwell) feels Austin's powers.

His ESP Proved SRO

Haley Joel Osment makes a large impact as *The Sixth Sense*'s small medium

Of the many ghostly and otherworldly films that proved a surprise draw at the multiplex, the biggest sensation was *The Sixth Sense,* which clung to the top of box office lists for five weeks. Helping to fuel that fascination was another surprise: Haley Joel Osment, the talented 11-year-old trouper who stars as Cole, a medium tormented by ghosts. Bruce Willis—who costars as the therapist who helps the boy come to terms with his megacase of ESP—ranks Haley "with some of the best adult actors I've ever worked with." In the business for more than half his young life, Osment was just 5 when he was spotted in the playroom of a Southern California furniture store and offered a Pizza Hut commercial. That in turn led to

the role of Forrest Jr. in the smash hit *Forrest Gump*.

Though the parts are rolling in these days—he also costarred in *The Jeff Foxworthy Show* and had a guest gig on *Ally McBeal*—success has not gone to Osment's head. Willis found him "immensely talented [yet] unaffected." At home in Glendale, California, with his father, actor Michael Eugene Osment, 34, mom Theresa, 30, a teacher, and sister Emily, 7, who also acts, Osment likes to shoot hoops and loves animals, particularly his mutt Sukie. When filming he has an on-set tutor, and, following in the footsteps of several modern-day child stars, Osment says, "I want to go to Yale to study drama." Any other ambitions? "I want to be one of those people who swims with the dolphins."

Don't See This Alone!

The Blair Witch Project rivets audiences with a dose of terror on the cheap

The ingredients sound about as promising as a grad school film project. Take a $30,000 budget, cast three unknown actors, pack them off into the Maryland woods for eight days with a handheld camera and a 35-page plot summary that contains no dialogue—then roll 'em. The resulting 81-minute film, *The Blair Witch Project,* proved a shocker on every front. After the largely black-and-white movie debuted at the Sundance Film Festival, then opened in July on just 27 screens, its tale of terror produced such deafening word-of-mouth raves that it was soon showing on 1,101 screens nationwide. The grainy horror film went on to gross $120 million, the largest haul ever for an indie movie.

Hollywood execs were also stunned that the priceless buzz was created without benefit of a costly advertising campaign. Instead, codirectors Daniel Myrick, 35, and Eduardo Sanchez, 30, and their marketers at Artisan Entertainment, designed a brilliant dot.com-era strategy. Its centerpiece, a Web site that cost just $15,000, drew 75 million hits—and that was just the first week.

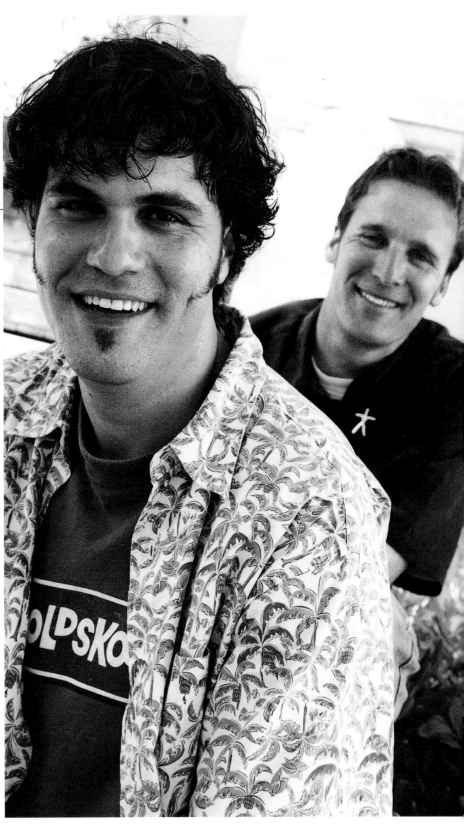

Sanchez (above, left) and Myrick made a name of the unheralded Heather Donahue (bottom).

The champ celebrated with bank manager wife Debbie, dog Fenway and his dad Thomas.

A Philbin Mil Goes to the IRS

His smash game show revives three dinosaurs—a network, a TV genre and Regis

"I saved ABC. Nobody but I could do that!" cracked TV vet Regis Philbin of his *Who Wants to Be a Millionaire,* the Americanization of a quirky British quiz show. It hit the airwaves for an August trial—and promptly won its time slot all 13 nights. Philbin, 68, was, in fact, not on the original list of host candidates until his agent schmoozed him into contention. In any case, *Millionaire* returned in November, boosting ABC's Nielsen sweep numbers by an awesome 30 percent, and a gold rush of copycat shows would follow on rival networks.

The climax came on November 18, when John Carpenter, 31, an IRS investigator from Hamden, Connecticut, won Philbin's first million-dollar jackpot with cyborgian sangfroid. A Trivial Pursuit addict, he had spent two semesters at Rutgers on academic probation before graduating into an interim job delivering Domino's pizza. A born ham, Carpenter appeared on Letterman's *Late Show, Saturday Night Live* and the cover of PEOPLE. "I could start over fresh," the childless Carpenter exulted, but he wasn't giving up his day job immediately. Indeed, his D.C. employer collected $400,000 of his bonanza.

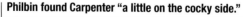

Philbin found Carpenter "a little on the cocky side."

Chamber Made

Judge Judy is the fastest, funniest mouth on TV

As all America rises for Judge Judy Sheindlin's fourth TV season of real-life small-claims cases, her menu of justice, tough love and common sense is crushing the competition from Oprah to Springer. With 9 million viewers, *Judge Judy* now boasts the largest audience of any syndicated daytime program. "This is some lark," says Sheindlin, 56, who is estimated to make $150,000 per week, plus profit participation. "My stress level is way down." Her newest rival is husband Jerry, 65, who presides over *The People's Court*. One too many gavels in the house? "Nah," says Jerry's lawyer daughter Nicole. "Double the fun."

She's in the Money

Financial guru Suze Orman helps readers be cash-savvy

Her message sounds New Age ("When you are powerful, money is attracted to you") crossed with *Investing for Dummies* (Look through your house for spare change, she advises). But when Suze Orman, 47, talks, wannabe millionaires listen. Her 1997 book *The 9 Steps to Financial Freedom* has 1.9 million copies in print, and spent nearly a year as America's bestselling advice book. But its weekly sales were immediately topped by her latest how-to tome, *The Courage to Be Rich*. Though she herself has to be loaded, Orman is hardly a spendthrift: She lives alone in the same one-bedroom home in Oakland Hills, California, that she bought 23 years ago.

Still Ready for Prime Time

Some old TV stars don't fade away. They only get brighter

RICK SCHRODER

Very few child stars move as ceaselessly and seamlessly into a successful adult career as Rick—formerly Ricky—Schroder. He began working before he could talk, shooting more than 60 commercials by the time he was 7. At 9, he made his movie debut in *The Champ,* holding the screen with Jon Voight and Faye Dunaway. Then, in the 1980s, he was Ricky Stratton (opposite Joel Higgins) on *Silver Spoons.* He went on to star in numerous TV movies, most famously *Lonesome Dove.* Still, all those credits didn't quiet skeptics when Schroder was tapped to play Det. Danny Sorenson, replacing Jimmy Smits' deceased Bobby Simone on *NYPD Blue.* But the New York City native had no problem with the authentic accent and attitude. A married father of three, Schroder, 29, now lives on and works a 45,000-acre ranch in Colorado, unconcerned by the weathering effects of the sun. Indeed, he seems proud of every wrinkle. "You won't see *me* get a face-lift," vows the onetime beautiful baby.

1983

1991

NEIL PATRICK HARRIS

Six-footer Neil Patrick Harris barely looks like Doogie Howser these days. And at 26, he's understandably tired of talking about the medical child prodigy he played from 1989 to 1993. After all, he's put together a substantial résumé since the saccharine series' demise—onstage in *Rent* and *Romeo and Juliet,* onscreen in *Starship Troopers,* on the tube in CBS's *Joan of Arc.* Now he's back to prime time in NBC's *Stark Raving Mad,* one of the season's successes. Harris plays a hyper, phobic book editor assigned to keep tabs on a testy horror novelist (Tony Shalhoub). It's a far cry from Doogie, which suits the unmarried amateur magician just fine. Harris, in fact, jokes that he shops for Howser memorabilia on the eBay auction site: "I'm trying to get it all for a big bonfire."

TYNE DALY

After two decades as a respected if little-known actress, Tyne Daly finally made her name and fame as Mary Beth Lacey, a no-nonsense New York City cop on CBS's *Cagney and Lacey.* Perfectly paired with Sharon Gless, Daly won four Emmys in the part. (Then, in 1996, she nabbed a record fifth as an actress in CBS's *Christy.*) After *C&L's* end in 1988, Daly risked a Broadway musical, *Gypsy,* and added a Tony. But her career took its toll. Her marriage to Georg Sanford Brown foundered in 1992, a year after she pleaded no contest to a drunk driving charge. Now she's back on the tube at 53, playing Amy Brenneman's prickly mother on CBS's *Judging Amy,* about which producer Barbara Hall bragged, "It's new to TV to have a strong female cast." Daly could disagree.

1983

Genie Uncorked

At 18, Christina Aguilera gets likened to Streisand

"All I want to do is be normal," sighs 18-year-old Christina Aguilera, pop's newest It girl. "But really, it's other people who won't let me be that way." When she attended her boyfriend's high school prom in suburban Pittsburgh, some girls gave her dirty looks, and when her hit single "Genie in a Bottle" came on, they stalked off the dance floor. But the 5'2" sensation with the serious pipes can ignore such pouting. She performed at 12 with Britney Spears at the Mickey Mouse Club in Orlando and in 1998 sang on the soundtrack of Disney's *Mulan*. Her first CD debuted at No. 1, elbowing aside a new Puff Daddy release. Now she's promoting her album, hobnobbing with stars like Jennifer Lopez and pondering buying a Porsche. She considers home Wexford, Pennsylvania—where her mom and sister moved post-divorce 12 years ago—but has a pad back in her native New York City. "If I was in school now," says Aguilera, "I'd be looking out of the window thinking, 'What if I'd gone out there to pursue my dream?'"

He's Still the Boss

Bruce Springsteen reunites with his band—and rules

"I can't promise you life everlasting," an elated, sweat-soaked Bruce Springsteen shouted at his adoring audience in East Rutherford, New Jersey. "But I can promise you life right now!" On this opening night of the reunited E Street Band's first U.S. tour in 10 years, he delivered, with three hours of ecstatic, full-throttle rock and roll. At 50, Springsteen lives comfortably on a sprawling estate in Rumson, New Jersey, with his second wife, backup singer Patti Scialfa, and their three kids, 16 miles—and a whole world—away from his blue-collar roots in Freehold. But strutting the stage with his sleeves rolled up, jabbing the air, roaring out his emotion-drenched anthems, the Boss electrified his fans as surely as when he rescued them from disco 25 years ago. When he left the stage, spent and exhilarated, they howled their homage: *Bruuuuce!*"

E Streeters (from left) Nils Lofgren, Clarence Clemons, Springsteen, Scialfa and Stevie Van Zandt proved that you can go home again.

The Beat Goes On

Racking up triumph after triumph, Cher proves her divahood is indestructible

For someone who's enjoyed as many showbiz incarnations as Elton John has pairs of funky glasses, Cher seemed to be singing a personal anthem when she recorded "Believe." But in typical Cher fashion, the unpredictable ensued: 35 years into her roller-coaster career, the original one-name wonder roared again to the top of the pop charts.

Still very much the provocative personality which she herself describes as "melancholy, hysterical, childish, strong and unusual," Cher (née Cherilyn Sarkisian) seems to be gathering momentum in midlife. The summer release of the artsy comedy *Tea with Mussolini* brought her the sort of respectful reviews the Best Actress Oscar winner (1987's *Moonstruck*) once only dreamed of.

In April she held her own with the likes of Tina Turner and Whitney Houston for *VH1 Divas Live '99*. During the concert, which drew 9.5 million TV viewers, Cher managed to out-diva the divas by creating the evening's only controversy: Did Cher only *lip-synch* the words to "Believe"? (She clearly sang her other numbers.) According to VH1 vice president Wayne Isaak, Cher did sing, but her effects-laden number was accompanied by a prerecorded "reinforcement track." It was much ado about little. Four months later, a telecast of her concert at the MGM Grand in Las Vegas proved that, at 52, Cher still has the voice, the supernova glow and the costuming that continues to confound.

Wise Guy with Worries

James Gandolfini makes his splash exposing the kinks of a Mafia kingpin

Whoever heard of a mobster who sees a shrink, takes Prozac, and frets about his weight, his wife, their kid? Nobody before HBO ventured *The Sopranos,* a brilliant series which earned 16 Emmy nominations in its very first season. "People respond to these flawed, fallible characters," says the show's inventor, David Chase. The conflicted capo on the couch and primo Soprano is Tony, played by balding, wide-bodied James Gandolfini, 37. As protective of his privacy as a real-life Godfather, Gandolfini explains, "I do a job. A carpenter does a job.

Edie Falco won an Emmy as his suffering wife.

He doesn't have to do an interview about the job he did." He will admit that he comes from "a nice Italian family from New Jersey," has two sisters, studied at Rutgers and now lives in New York City. He worked as a nightclub manager and a truck driver for a company called Gimme Seltzer, got noticed in *True Romance* and *Get Shorty,* and became a public face in *The Sopranos.* Recently, he says, "some homeless guy yells, 'Hey Tony!' and I wondered, 'How does this guy know who I am? Does he have HBO or what?'"

Catch 'Em All!

Pokémon mania sweeps prepubescent America

It began modestly in Japan in 1996 as a handheld video game—a technology that was already being eclipsed in America by more sophisticated CD-ROM software. But the 151 colorful creatures that make up the Pokémon menagerie proved so seductive that Japan was soon saturated with Pokémon comic books, trading cards, toys, even a TV series. Never mind that the appeal of the little Pocket Monsters— part cuddly Teletubby, part avenging Power Ranger—was lost on anyone under 5 or over 15. Nintendo saw the potential, and did what any sane marketer would do: It retooled the phenomenon for the lucrative, fad-mad American market. Since invading U.S. shores in late '98, Pokémon has produced an estimated $6 billion bonanza. The trading cards alone have generated $300 million in sales—not to mention schoolyard fights and lawsuits. The *Pokémon* series, which airs six days a week on the WB network, is top rated. The week *Pokémon: The First Movie* hit theaters, it topped box office charts. Adults pretty much don't get any of this—which pretty much might be the point.

Spell Binder

Britain's J.K. Rowling enchants with her tales starring a young wizard

For author J.K. Rowling, it all started on a 1990 train trip as she was traveling from Manchester to London. "I was staring out the window and the idea for Harry just came," says Rowling, 33. "The basic idea was for a boy who didn't know what he was." Harry may have been in the dark, but readers on six continents now know all about the lad who discovers he is a wizard. The British author's first three books in a planned series of seven—*Harry Potter and the Sorcerer's Stone, Harry Potter and the Chamber of Secrets, Harry Potter and the Prisoner of Azkaban*—simultaneously held the top three slots on the *New York Times'* bestseller list while *Sorcerer's Stone* went to No. 1 on the paperback charts.

Not bad for a divorced mom who, following the birth of her daughter Jessica in 1993, wound up on welfare. She moved to Edinburgh to be near her sister Di, and remembers being "stuck in an appalling poverty trap." But she had already written three chapters about Harry and crafted much of the rest in cafes, pram by her side, to escape her grotty flat. Her initial attempts in 1995 to sell *Sorcerer's Stone* met with rejection slips. Finally, literary agent Christopher Little sold it to Bloomsbury Press for about $4,000, and one reviewer compared her to Roald Dahl. Now the bewitching series is selling by the millions, film rights have been optioned, and Rowling is reported to have earned $14 million.

Little Sis's Big Score

Serena Williams, not Venus, took the U.S. Open—and at 17

"I didn't know if I should laugh, cry or scream," said 17-year-old tennis phenom Serena Williams. "So I did them all." The 5'11", 145-lb. powerhouse had just scored a thrilling upset of No. 1 seed Martina Hingis in the September finals of the U.S. Open. The victory made her the first black woman to win the Open since Althea Gibson in 1958 as well as the only African-American besides Arthur Ashe to win a Grand Slam singles title in the last quarter century. Another surprise was that Serena was the first of five Williams sisters to break through. Originally the family hope was Venus, 19, a finalist in the 1997 Open. Indeed, Venus had pushed Hingis into a draining third set in the semis the day before, and that gave Serena some possible advantage and "even more motivation, because I could win for both of us."

The Williamses were toughened by their start on run-down public courts in Compton, a gang-ridden suburb of Los Angeles. Their outspoken father, Richard, ran a private security firm; their mother, Oracene, was a nurse. "They were always super nice, polite kids," recalls Rick Macci, a former coach, who reported that Serena is "a little more happy-go-lucky than Venus." The new family champ fielded a call from President Clinton and volleyed with Katie Couric (among other talk show appearances). She tools to the mall in her yellow BMW Z3, with a Tweety Bird antenna ornament, and is building a house near the family home in Palm Beach Gardens, Florida. Her roommate will be sister Venus, with whom she also won the 1999 U.S. Open doubles championship and, most amazingly of all, claims not to have fought since she was 6.

On Tiger's Tail

At 19, Sergio Garcia erupts as a golf superstar

Yes, he did have to withdraw from the St. Jude Classic in Memphis because of a severe acne attack, but otherwise golf sensation Sergio Garcia can handle a skins competition with his elders. That's about everybody, because he is only 19. Four months after the freckle-faced Spaniard turned pro, he finished a dramatic, hard-charging second to Tiger Woods in the U.S. PGA and became the youngest player ever in the prestigious Ryder Cup. His father is a club pro, and Garcia was practically born on the links: His mother, who runs the club's pro shop, was helping at a tournament when she went into labor. Sergio began practicing his swing with a broom at age 2 and proclaimed his desire to be "No. 1 in the world" when he was 14. "Sergio has charisma," says Woods, clearly feeling the breeze from the kid now known as El Niño.

Like any other jittery couple, Sophie had lost 10 pounds and Edward had difficulty getting the ring over her knuckle. But, of course, they took their vows before a TV audience of 200 million.

Windsor Castle Rocks

Formality gyrates out the window as Prince Edward weds Sophie Rhys-Jones

This was a very different royal wedding from that other one 18 years ago. Prince Edward, 35, the Queen's youngest son, strolled out of Windsor Castle flanked by his smiling brothers, Charles and Andrew. All three wore morning suits instead of the customary military regalia. Inside the chapel, the bride, a public relations executive (and commoner), Sophie Rhys-Jones, 34, was waiting in a sophisticated silk coatdress, along with family, friends and a minimum of dignitaries. Unlike Diana, Sophie got her groom's names right—Edward Antony Richard Louis—but neglected to kiss the guy. (They did, however, smooch in private.) Like the late princess, Sophie had already been exposed to a withering media barrage, culminating in a topless photo in a London tabloid. But all that was forgotten at the happy, rowdy party after the ceremony. As the Royal Marines Band thundered through selected rock oldies, royals of all generations boogied, with Prince William leading the line dancing, and the Queen Mother doing a spirited twist at 99. The Earl and Countess of Wessex (titles they assumed on their wedding day) will have a royal estate near Windsor, and try to live a normal existence—he as a TV producer, she back at her firm and away from him part of the workweek. But for the bride, nothing will be the same. Said a colleague after the wedding: "Sophie was glowing. It was like she was being beamed into another life."

Falling in Love Again

Princess Caroline hopes that her third marriage try, to a prince, will be the charm

She was a lesser if more famous noble than he—Ernst August of Hanover—and as a descendant of Britain's King George III and Germany's Kaiser Wilhelm II, the prince required Queen Elizabeth's permission to marry Princess Caroline of Monaco. The Queen consented, and on January 23, Caroline, who turned 42 that day, and Ernst, 44, exchanged vows in a low-key civil ceremony in Monaco's pink palace, before a small group of friends and family, including Caroline's 75-year-old dad, Prince Rainier, and the couple's five combined offspring. Noticeably absent was Caroline's estranged sister Stephanie.

It was a brave and hopeful new beginning for a princess whose life has been no fairy tale. She divorced her philandering first husband in 1980 and lost her mother,

Princess Grace, two years later. In 1990 her second husband was killed in a speedboat accident. In the years that followed, Caroline grew closer to Ernst, whom she'd known since her teens. It was Ernst who comforted her in 1995 when a condition called alopecia caused her hair to fall out. Of course, no one pals with a Grimaldi without press attention, and Ernst's then wife soon began divorce proceedings. After the divorce became final in 1997, Caroline and Ernst went public. He still wasn't used to the paparazzi and has assaulted one photographer with his umbrella (and paid damages). Yet friends say this is a good match. The two share a love of parties, art and children. And right on cue, six months after the nuptials, Princess Alexandra was born.

Makeover Champ of the Year

Sarah Ferguson gets out of both the red and, for now anyway, the royal hair

Sarah Ferguson, Duchess of York, has dug herself out of a financial hole and, finally at 40, achieved a measure of self-knowledge. As a spokeswoman for Weight Watchers (worth $1 million a year) and Wedgwood ($750,000), the newly slimmed-down "special correspondent" for NBC's *Today* show ($600,000) has finally cleared her $7.1 million in debts. Now her biggest problem is finding time to spend at Sunninghill Park, the home she and daughters Beatrice, 11, and Eugenie, 9, share amicably with ex-husband Andrew. "I don't like this busyness. I'm a Libra—I like harmony," the Duchess says ruefully.

For a long time, harmony seemed the last word you'd associate with flame-haired Fergie, with her girlish, over-the-top naughtiness that pleased only Fleet Street and capsized her marriage. Hard times followed, as she suffered the royal cold shoulder. The Windsors gave her a meager divorce settlement of only $495,000 plus child support, as opposed to Diana's $28 million, and cut her out of their lives. But Fergie pulled herself together, buoyed by the steady, seemingly surprising affection of her ex and a two-year involvement with an Italian nobleman. "I quite like the person I am," she says. "I'd like her as a friend."

The Shrinking Shadow of Diana

Wills rows his boat, Camilla and Charles cruise in one, and Hewitt fails to rock it

Case Closed, Finally

After two long years of investigation, French authorities concluded that the Mercedes-Benz carrying Princess Diana, 36, and Dodi Fayed, 42, careened in a Paris tunnel because the driver, Henri Paul, 41, was drunk and on prescription drugs at the time of the crash that also killed him. The report said that the princess and Fayed (shown at the Ritz Hotel just before entering the car) would have survived if they'd latched their seat belts.

A Once-a-Year Crown

First year at Eton has been a breeze for Prince Harry, 14, who donned a Nepalese Sherpa hat on the school's charity day, when students pay £1 to abandon their normal formal duds. After struggling with his studies since his mother's death, the young prince seems to be coming into his own.

The Cad Who Wouldn't Shut Up

"The most reviled man in Britain" is how the tabloids describe James Hewitt, 41, blabby former cavalry officer and lover of Princess Diana. Dumped from the army after failing the test for major in 1993, Hewitt opened a riding school which failed, leaving him strapped for cash. So he essayed a second memoir of their five-year affair (the first was published in 1994), which had little to add, because the law prevented his including Diana's love notes. Basically, he reiterates that the princess made the first move, that he still loves her and that no, he was not the sire of Prince Harry.

Wills on the Move

At Eton, Prince William (center), 17, crews, captains the swim team and plays rugby (leading to the fracture of an index finger). At home, he dates and goes clubbing with Tom Parker Bowles, 24. (Tom is Camilla's son and the godson of Charles, who reportedly called him a "bloody fool" for trying cocaine.)

Charles and Camilla Go Public as a Pair

Three years after his divorce and two after Diana's death, Prince Charles, 50, and his longtime love, Camilla Parker Bowles, 51, made their first official public appearance—at a fête at London's Ritz Hotel. It included a carefully choreographed, 20-second photo op and proved a sort of dress rehearsal for a Mediterranean cruise together; a solo, five-day meet-the-glitterati tour of New York City for her; and a joint entertainment at Buckingham Palace (while Mum was away). Even if Camilla will never be queen herself, Charles is treating her like one, reputedly ponying up $247,500 a year for her expenses.

Isn't It Bliss? Well, So Far

Raquel takes the fourth; Courteney, Helen, Shannon and a Spice venture their first

Actors **COURTENEY COX**, 35, and **DAVID ARQUETTE**, 27, were both styled by Valentino for their San Francisco wedding.

The honeymoon ended for a Broadway theater scion when his bride of five months, **JESSICA SKLAR**, 28, a Tommy Hilfiger PR, dumped him in '98 and later accepted a proposal from career bachelor **JERRY SEINFELD**, 45, in a chic Gotham bistro.

When Olympic gymnast **SHANNON MILLER**, 22, landed medical resident **CHRIS PHILLIPS**, 26, six of the 13 bridesmaids were Miller's 1996 teammates, including Kerri Strug, Dominique Dawes and Dominique Moceanu.

Brat Packer emeritus **MOLLY RINGWALD**, 31, wed her longtime French-novelist amour, **VALÉRY LAMEIGNÈRE**, 33, in Bordeaux.

Fourth-time bride **RAQUEL WELCH**, 58, married pizza parlor owner **RICHIE PALMER**, 44, in a gown to indicate how well her iconic cleavage is holding up.

Basketball ace **GRANT HILL**, 26, hooked up with rhythm-and-blues singer **TAMIA**, 24, in Battle Creek, Michigan.

Actress **ROSIE PEREZ**, 34, shared legal and "spiritual" rites with longtime beau **SETH ZVI ROSENFELD**, 36, a filmmaker.

After a five-year courtship, actors **HANK AZARIA**, 35, and **HELEN HUNT**, 36, tied the knot in a traditional Jewish service.

Actor **GREG KINNEAR**, 35, wed writer **HELEN LABDON**, 29, in her native England.

Actress **JULIETTE LEWIS** and pro skateboarder **STEVE BERRA**, both 26, staged their ceremony by a waterfall on a hillside in Big Sur, California, at dusk.

With his three kids as witnesses, *Starship Troopers'* **CASPER VAN DIEN**, 30, wed *Dynasty's* **CATHERINE OXENBERG**, 37, at a Las Vegas wedding chapel.

VICTORIA ADAMS (a.k.a. Posh Spice), 25, and soccer star **DAVID BECKHAM**, 24, sat on thrones, with their 4-month-old in between.

New Divas Enter the Building

When a budding star arrives in the house, even the most blasé celebs go all goo-goo

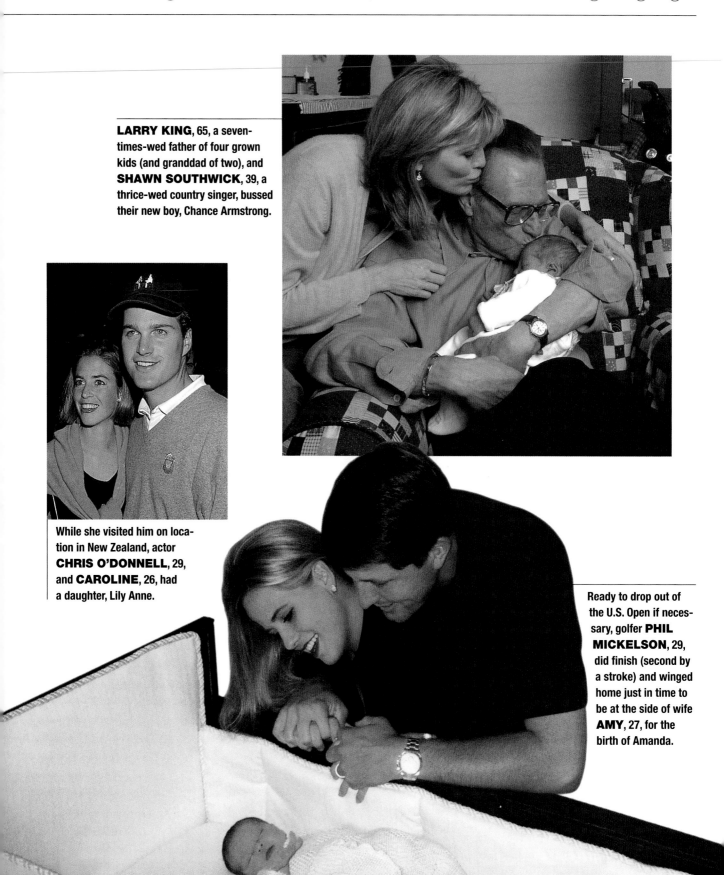

LARRY KING, 65, a seven-times-wed father of four grown kids (and granddad of two), and **SHAWN SOUTHWICK**, 39, a thrice-wed country singer, bussed their new boy, Chance Armstrong.

While she visited him on location in New Zealand, actor **CHRIS O'DONNELL**, 29, and **CAROLINE**, 26, had a daughter, Lily Anne.

Ready to drop out of the U.S. Open if necessary, golfer **PHIL MICKELSON**, 29, did finish (second by a stroke) and winged home just in time to be at the side of wife **AMY**, 27, for the birth of Amanda.

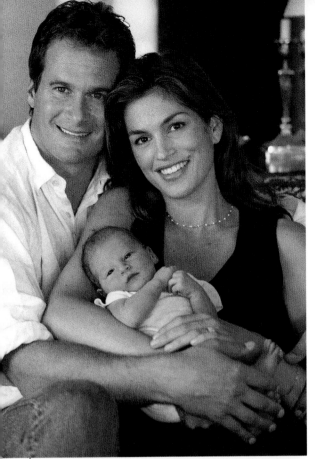

Born at home in Los Angeles, Presley Walker Gerber basked in the beauteous genes of parents **CINDY CRAWFORD**, 33, and nightclub owner **RANDE GERBER**, 37.

Spice Girl (Scary) **MELANIE BROWN**, 23, strutted relatively sveltely just weeks before the arrival of daughter Phoenix by dancer hubby Jimmy Gulzar, 32.

Midas (or monopolist?), Microsoft's **BILL GATES**, 43, and wife **MELINDA**, 34, had a second child, Rory John.

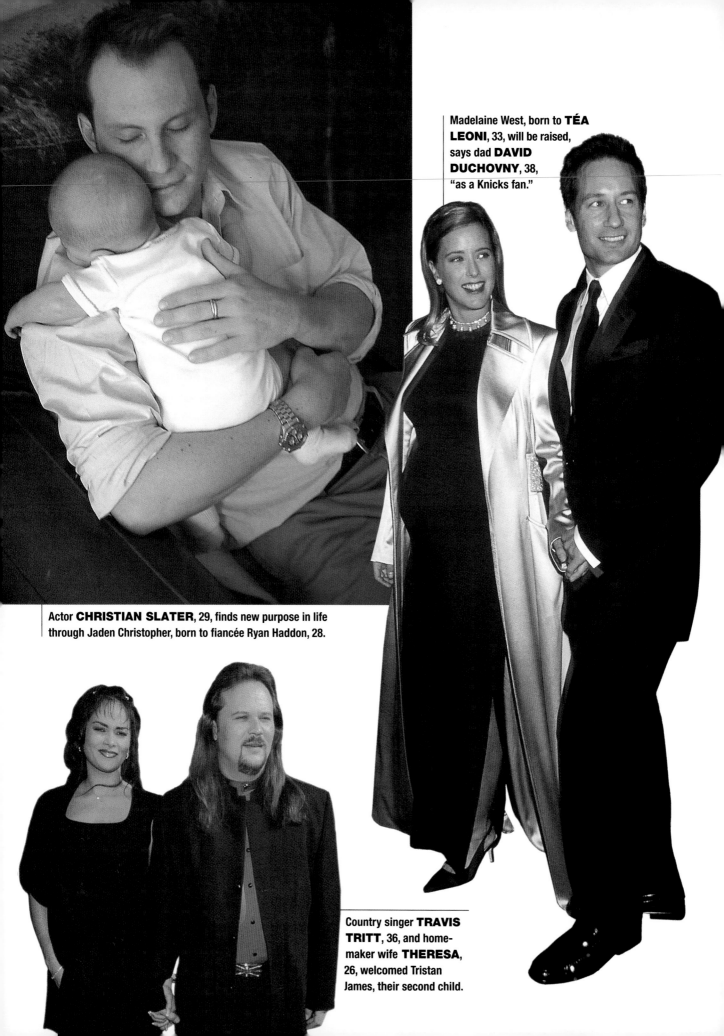

Madelaine West, born to **TÉA LEONI**, 33, will be raised, says dad **DAVID DUCHOVNY**, 38, "as a Knicks fan."

Actor **CHRISTIAN SLATER**, 29, finds new purpose in life through Jaden Christopher, born to fiancée Ryan Haddon, 28.

Country singer **TRAVIS TRITT**, 36, and home-maker wife **THERESA**, 26, welcomed Tristan James, their second child.

Baby Matthew makes it a lucky seven for talk show host **MARIE OSMOND**, 39, and record producer Brian Blosil, 46.

Ally McBeal's **GIL BELLOWS**, 31, cut the umbilical cord of Ava Emanuelle, born to his wife, Rya Kihlstedt, 29.

AL ROKER, 44, *Today's* weatherman, and *20/20's* **DEBORAH ROBERTS**, 38, dote on their first, Leila Ruth, born in late '98.

In Los Angeles, two months after their wedding, actors **REESE WITHERSPOON**, 23, and Ryan Phillippe, 25, greeted daughter Ava Elizabeth.

A Century Ended in a Split Parade

It was game, set, mismatch for Andre and Brooke and predictably for Mick Jagger. But Amy Grant?

Her 16-year union over with songwriter **GARY CHAPMAN**, 41, Christian singer **AMY GRANT**, 38, linked up with C&W star Vince Gill, 47.

Long-suffering **JERRY HALL**, 42, finally ended her storm-tossed 21-year saga after a 28-year-old Brazilian model said she was preggers by **MICK JAGGER**, 55.

After not quite two years of marriage (and only about six weeks of cohabitation), **ANDRE AGASSI**, 29, and **BROOKE SHIELDS**, 33, called it splits.

College sweetheart **LAURA DEIBLE**, 43, stuck with **TIM ALLEN**, 46, through his cocaine imprisonment and sudden stardom, only to see their 15-year marriage collapse when Allen stopped shooting *Home Improvement*.

Following the public meltdown of her engagement to Brad Pitt, **GWYNETH PALTROW** hooked up with *Shakespeare in Love* costar **BEN AFFLECK**, also 26. But shortly after their movie smash opened, they discreetly parted.

They met as Gap models, wed in 1987 and, three kids later, actress **ANDIE MacDOWELL** and contractor **PAUL QUALLEY**, both 41, announced a separation.

"I hope and pray she will come back," said **ROD STEWART**, 54, when model **RACHEL HUNTER**, 29, split after eight years and two kids.

TRISHA YEARWOOD, 35, and Mavericks bassist **ROBERT REYNOLDS**, 37, went kaput 5¹/₂ years after their Ryman Auditorium wedding.

Year 13 was all they wrote for **JANET JACKSON**, 32, and boyfriend **RENÉ ELIZONDO JR.**, 36, co-lyricist on her last three LP hits.

Romance novelist **DANIELLE STEEL**, 52, was cut adrift after 17 months with yachtsman Tom Perkins, 67, her fifth husband.

"No one else was involved," declared **HELENA BONHAM CARTER**, 33, as she ended six years with Emma Thompson's ex, **KENNETH BRANAGH**, 38.

Subordinates address her as Miss Ross, and **DIANA ROSS**, 55, is just that again after 13 years with shipping tycoon **ARNE NAESS**, 61.

His workaholism doomed the three-year relationship of **GEORGE CLOONEY**, 38, and French model **CÉLINE BALITRAN**, 24. His new roomie: a 150-lb. potbellied pig named Max.

JOE DI MAGGIO

The loneliest hero, the Yankee Clipper
played for the crowd but never to it

I n the winter of 1954, just weeks after marrying Joe DiMaggio, Marilyn Monroe interrupted their honeymoon in Tokyo to entertain U.S. troops in Korea. The servicemen greeted her wildly. "Joe," she told him upon her return, "you've never heard such cheering." "Yes," responded DiMaggio, "I have." Indeed. And for the baseball Hall of Famer, the cheering kept on coming at Old-Timers' Games, celebrity golf tourneys and autograph shows almost until the day he died at 84 in Hollywood, Florida, of complications from lung cancer.

The eighth of nine children (including two major league brothers) of a Northern California fishing family, DiMaggio came to the New York Yankees for $25,000 in 1936 as a gawky, toothy high school dropout, but by the time he left the game in 1951, he had become the sport's exemplar of elegance and grace. His stats—a .325 career batting average, three MVP awards, an epic 56-game hitting streak in 1941—were matched by his style. Fans will never forget his fluid swing or the way his lean, 6'2" form seemed to glide over the vast outfield at Yankee Stadium. In his 15 years there, the team won nine world championships. Yet even more remarkable was the way his legend blossomed in retirement. Rarely granting interviews, he projected an aloof, mythic dignity hymned in the Paul Simon lyric "A nation turns its lonely eyes to you."

Solitude was no stranger to DiMaggio. His marriage to Hollywood starlet Dorothy Arnold, mother of his only child, lasted barely five years. He met Monroe on a blind date in 1952, and he likened their chemistry to "a good double-play combination." She reported being equally impressed, because "he didn't make a pass at me right away." They married in 1954 at San Francisco's city hall. The public went wild over the union of the magisterial slugger and the sex goddess, but the two were painfully ill-matched. Testifying in their divorce proceedings, Monroe characterized DiMaggio as a moody sort who often snapped "Leave me alone!" when she asked what the trouble was. The marriage was over within nine months, and yet they remained friends until Monroe's death in 1962. DiMaggio famously refused to discuss her, never remarried and sent roses to her grave three times a week for the next 20 years. "He lived a very, very lonely life for a long time," said author David Halberstam.

His tight group of family and friends saw a kinder, easier DiMaggio, one who loved John Ford westerns and Barbra Streisand's voice. But there were ground rules. "It wasn't easy being part of Joe's inner circle," notes New York City physician Rock Positano, a longtime pal. "There was always a tremendous amount of responsibility and stress. You couldn't even bring a friend to dinner without clearing it with Joe first." Though his relationship with son Joe III was strained and they remained unreconciled at the time of his death, DiMaggio doted on his two granddaughters and four great-grandchildren. "One day he calls

Marilyn Monroe (in the mid-1950s) was surely the love of his life, but she was also his "heartbreak," believed pal Bill Fugazy.

and says, 'I need a favor,'" Positano recalls. "'Do you think you could get me a Beanie Baby?'"

Aside from occasional TV commercials, DiMaggio spent most of his postbaseball years simply being Joe DiMaggio. He was aware of his status, insisting that he be introduced at Old-Timers' Games as "baseball's greatest living player," a distinction voted him by a group of sportswriters in 1969. For his appearances at golf events and autograph signings, he commanded large fees. Yet there were some things he did free of charge. In his last years he raised millions for the Joe DiMaggio Children's Hospital near his Florida home and visited the 144-bed facility regularly. During an appearance at the hospital in September he met Allison Bine, 12, who had cystic fibrosis. Her grandfather Stanley Bine remembers, "You felt very comfortable in his presence." DiMaggio entered another wing of the same facility a month later and spent 99 days battling his illness. Then he went home to die. At the end, granddaughters and a brother were by his side. "His face was radiant the moment he died," says hospice nurse Javier Ribe. "He looked as young as the first picture I remember seeing of him. So peaceful, so peaceful."

DiMaggio's estranged son, Joe III, died five months later at 57 in what turned out to be a year of loss for the world of baseball. Pee Wee Reese, the great Brooklyn shortstop of the 1950s who struck a blow for racial tolerance when he put his arm around teammate Jackie Robinson in front of a jeering Cincinnati crowd, succumbed to lung cancer at 80. He was followed by Catfish Hunter, the hard-throwing pitcher of the 1970s and the first multimillionaire free agent, dead at 53 of Lou Gehrig's disease. But in the black-and-white film and sepia stills, these legends remain at the top of their game and forever young.

Children were his one cause beside his image, and in the more innocent 1940, DiMag gave away his autograph gratis.

OSEOLA MCCARTY

Her six-figure scholarship gift taught the world a gentle lesson in selflessness

She had a simple philosophy that she would articulate when pressed: "If you can help somebody, help them." But for most of her 91 years, Mississippi washerwoman Oseola McCarty was more inclined to let her actions do the talking. In 1995 she delivered a particularly eloquent message when she donated $150,000 to the University of Southern Mississippi to establish a scholarship fund for African-American students. Her generosity so touched people the world over that the unassuming laundress became a cultural hero and was given the Presidential Citizens Medal by Bill Clinton.

Growing up in Hattiesburg, McCarty was a lonely only child who dreamed of a future in nursing until she had to quit the sixth grade to spend a year caring for a sick aunt. Convinced that she'd fallen too far behind to catch up, McCarty joined her mother and grandmother at the washboard. Hardworking and frugal, McCarty, whose fee gradually rose from 50 cents to $10 a bundle, somehow put away $250,000. "Her giving $150,000," says university president Horace W. Fleming Jr., "was the equivalent of the wealthy giving a billion." Childless and never married, she left behind (after dying from liver cancer) a fund in her name, now worth $330,000, that has already provided full scholarships to nine undergraduates.

The man of reflection (in 1974) found fulfillment with Princess Raiyah and Queen Noor (in 1998) and in the Wye settlement with Arafat, Clinton and Netanyahu.

KingHussein

A skillful navigator of Mideast enmities and egos, he relentlessly pursued peace

He was the only ruler most Jordanians ever knew. So when non-Hodgkin's lymphoma ended the 46-year reign of King Hussein at the age of 63, his 4.5 million subjects took it like a death in the family. "I feel like some part of me is lost," said shopkeeper Indrous Habib, one of 800,000 mourners who crowded the streets of Amman for the king's funeral. Fittingly, the many world leaders who attended—from President Clinton to Israeli premier Benjamin Netanyahu—shared that sense of loss for the man who had toiled so tenaciously for peace in the Middle East. Hussein's was a life of outsize drama. In 1951, he was at his grandfather Abdullah's side when the monarch was slain. At 17, he ascended to the throne after his own father's rule was cut short by schizophrenia. Over the decades, Hussein would escape more than a dozen assassination attempts, and he left the Mayo Clinic after cancer treatments to help seal the 1998 Wye agreement. A man of considerable charm and a roving eye, Hussein had 12 children by four wives. His final union, to Queen Noor (née Lisa Halaby of Washington, D.C.), lasted 20 blissful years.

AL HIRT
A big man with an even bigger sound, he was known as the King of the Trumpet

Though the first horn he acquired at age 6 was purchased from a pawnshop, there was nothing secondhand about Al Hirt's sound. In a career that spanned six decades, the rotund Dixieland trumpeter, whom friends called Jumbo, produced 55 albums that along the way garnered 21 Grammy nominations and won the 1963 award in the non-jazz instrumental category. "I'm a pop commercial musician," he often explained, "I'm not a jazz trumpet."

After launching his career with the big bands that dominated the 1940s, including those led by Tommy Dorsey and Benny Goodman, Hirt started his own band in the '50s, then went on to achieve such popularity in the '60s that he was invited to play at John F. Kennedy's Inaugural ball. Then, in 1967, he headlined the half-time show of pro football's first Super Bowl, the first of five such appearances. In 1987 he performed Handel's "Ave Maria" during the visit of Pope John Paul II to Hirt's beloved New Orleans.

The son of a Big Easy police officer, Hirt polished his technique at the Cincinnati Conservatory of Music but honed his robust and distinctive sound in the clubs of the French Quarter, where he ran a jazz club on Bourbon Street for almost a quarter of a century. Twice married, with 6 children, 10 grandchildren and 2 great-grandkids, Hirt died of liver failure at 76 at his New Orleans home. Clarinetist Pete Fountain, who grew up with Hirt in the local clubs, eulogized, "When you say Al Hirt, you say New Orleans; when you say New Orleans, you say Al Hirt."

DUSTY SPRINGFIELD
A London convent girl with a towering hairdo and a killer voice became a pop star and gay icon

Burt Bacharach dubbed her the White Queen of Soul. It was the perfect title for Dusty Springfield. Her look was regal, from the platinum bouffant hairdos to the panda eyes ringed with makeup. Her voice—smoky, sensual and aching with emotion—was pure torch. Starting out as a folkie with her group the Springfields, the former Mary Isabel Catherine Bernadette O'Brien went solo in 1963, recording such smash singles as "I Only Want to Be with You," "You Don't Have to Say You Love Me" and "Son of a Preacher Man." But her 1969 album *Dusty in Memphis* crowned a success she couldn't sustain. Drinking and cocaine problems ensued, and her moodiness alienated fellow musicians and record producers. After going public with her bisexuality in the 1970s, Springfield became a heroine among gays, and her comeback recording, 1987's *What Have I Done to Deserve This,* with the Pet Shop Boys, engaged a new generation of fans. She learned of her induction into the Rock and Roll Hall of Fame just before her death at 59, following a five-year battle with breast cancer. She left "a legacy of beautiful recordings and fabulous memories," said her friend Elton John. "At her funeral . . . as the coffin came out of the Henley-on-Thames church, she had a standing ovation."

STANLEY KUBRICK

From his closed sets and countless takes came a cinema treasure trove

"One man writes a symphony," Stanley Kubrick once said. "It is essential for one man to make a film." Just weeks after finishing his long-awaited erotic thriller *Eyes Wide Shut,* he died of a heart attack at 70. The famously obsessive director who apprenticed as a still photographer had composed just 13 celluloid symphonies, a mere 9 of them in the last four decades.

Kubrick's movies tackled substantial themes like the tyranny of technology and the power of the state over individuals. Yet his films were often immensely commercial, and more than a few became classics, including the antiwar epic *Paths of Glory* (1957), the black comedy *Dr. Strangelove* (1964), the trippy, speculative *2001: A Space Odyssey* (1968) and the garishly violent *A Clockwork Orange* (1971).

Kubrick stopped giving interviews years ago and filmed in total secrecy. His last three works were created near the 19-room manor north of London where the New York City native had retreated with artist Christiane Harlan, his third wife and mother of his three

DIRK BOGARDE

A British matinee idol outgrew light film comedy to leave behind a deeper, darker body of work

He was called the British Rock Hudson in the 1950s, but the dashing star began to venture beyond romantic comedy when he was cast in 1961's *Victim,* one of the first movies to tackle the then-taboo subject of homosexuality. By the time Dirk Bogarde died of a heart attack at 78, he had become celebrated for his sensitive, multi-dimensional performances in innovative movies like *The Servant, Darling* and *Accident.* Perhaps his most famous role was that of the doomed composer von Aschenbach in the film version of Thomas Mann's *Death in Venice* (1971). A quiet man who mistrusted fame, Bogarde became a writer and lived in the South of France with Anthony Forward, his manager and companion of 40 years.

daughters. Fearing high speeds, he insisted his chauffeur drive his vintage Rolls no faster than 30 mph. But Kubrick's mind, noted friend John le Carré, "was always whizzing along. He was a vacuum cleaner." A most meticulous one. He would shoot as many as 100 takes to polish a minor scene, but actors like Tom Cruise and Nicole Kidman gladly gave up months to join him. Putting up with Kubrick's perfectionism was the price of working for the artist Steven Spielberg called "the grand master of filmmaking."

ANTHONYNEWLEY

He conquered a bleak childhood,
Broadway and, briefly, Joan Collins

Anthony Newley's feverish drive began in Hackney, a working-class London neighborhood. Born illegitimate and raised by a single mother, "he was starved of approval," says pal Herbert Kretzmer, lyricist for *Les Misérables*. After joining an acting class, Newley tasted success at 16 as the Artful Dodger in David Lean's brilliant 1948 film adaptation of *Oliver Twist*. In 1961 he teamed with Leslie Bricusse to write songs and musicals, in which Newley figured he could cast himself. A year later he bestrode Broadway after writing, directing and starring in *Stop the World—I Want to Get Off,* in which he played a Chaplinesque everyman. "Anthony," says Bricusse, "had a bit of the tragic clown in him."

Though Newley never clicked as a Hollywood actor, he wrote some of filmdom's more memorable tunes, among them "Goldfinger" and "The Candy Man," Sammy Davis Jr.'s trademark song. Newley, who had three ex-wives, including actress Joan Collins, and four children, died of cancer at 67. His painful final days were brightened by British designer Gina Fratini, with whom he'd had a two-year affair in the 1950s and reunited with in 1993.

RICHARD KILEY

His 50-year career was quixotic in the best sense

Richard Kiley's wife, Patricia, said he considered himself "a character man in a leading man's body," and he proved it in films like *Blackboard Jungle* and TV's *The Thornbirds.* But above all, "he loved being on the stage," says Patricia. By the time Kiley died at 76 of myelodysplasia, he'd won two Tonys, including one for his classic role, Don Quixote in *Man of La Mancha* (with Ray Middleton, right). When "The Impossible Dream" was played at his funeral, said his wife, "we all lost it."

GENE SISKEL

A popular critic, he kept the movie industry under his thumb

The skinny, boyishly enthusiastic half of the team returned typically to his workaholic regimen after surgery for a brain tumor, taping PBS's *Siskel & Ebert at the Movies,* reviewing for the *Chicago Tribune* and *TV Guide* and appearing on *CBS This Morning.* Eight months later, Siskel died at 53, ending a quarter century trading opinions and acerbic quips with portly *Chicago Sun-Times* rival Roger Ebert, 56, as they graded the week's flicks with their trademark thumbs-up or -down. "We both thought we were the other's older or smarter brother," said Ebert. A man of passion, Siskel was mad for his wife of 19 years, Marlene Iglitzen, their three kids, the Chicago Bulls and, unlike some reviewers, the movies. He saw *Saturday Night Fever* at least 17 times and paid $2,000 for John Travolta's white disco suit.

VICTOR MATURE

A beefy he-man with a sense of humor, he grinned all the way to the bank

Few movie musclemen have combined a .45 caliber wit with the 45" chest that Victor Mature displayed in such barely clothed epics as *Samson and Delilah* (with Hedy Lamarr) and *The Robe* (with Jean Simmons). "I was casting about for a job where a guy without brains could make more money than the President," he once cracked. During his glamorous Hollywood run, Mature, who died of leukemia at 86, made some 70 films and reigned as the preeminent hunk of his day.

Born in Louisville, Kentucky, the son of an Austrian scissors grinder turned refrigerator executive, Mature was a rebellious youth who dropped out at 15 after getting himself thrown out of four schools. Famous for dating luminaries like Rita Hayworth and Lana Turner, he had five wives, and with the last one, Lorey Sabena, he produced a daughter, Victoria, 24, an opera singer like her mother.

Hardly a mindless pinup boy, Mature had a knack for making a nickel. By selling TV sets from his *Samson* dressing room, he began a profitable business that endured well past his screen career and enabled him to retire to San Diego at 46 to play golf. "There's a lot to be said for loafing if you know how to do it gracefully," he once said. Piper Laurie, one of his many costars, recalls, "He was just this great hunk of sensuality." To such sentiments Mature had a swift comeback: "I don't mind being called Glamor Boy, as long as that check comes on Friday."

MEL TORMÉ
The Velvet Fog wrote 'Born to Be Blue' but painted the show world and the town red

A prolific and protean artist, Mel Tormé was not only a jazz singer with a scat skill like that of Ella Fitzgerald but also an accomplished drummer, pianist, arranger, actor and author of several books and some 300 songs, among them "The Christmas Song (Chestnuts Roasting on an Open Fire . . .)."

Born in Chicago to Russian immigrants, he caught fire as a crooner in the 1940s after a New York City deejay gave him a nickname, the Velvet Fog, that Tormé came to detest. He faded in the 1960s, a victim of rock, but found a new audience appearing on TV's *Night Court.* "I just loved his enthusiasm," recalled Harry Anderson, the show's Tormé-fan star. It obviously extended to his love life, which included a fling with Ava Gardner, three divorces and five children before he settled down in 1984 with attorney Ali Severson. "Absence," he said of his road life, "makes the heart go wander." Tormé was confined to a wheelchair by a 1996 stroke, but until he finally died at 73, he never missed Monday nights at Hugh Hefner's mansion. One of his last recordings was a duet on "Straighten Up and Fly Right" with his son Steve. "I brought it over to his house," says Steve. "He sat there with this smile, and he just had tears running down his face. So I think he liked it."

ALLEN FUNT

His placing real folks in weird situations with a hidden camera was cruel but cool

Allen Funt was so famous that when a plane he flew on was hijacked to Cuba in 1969, his fellow passengers assumed it was just another Funt stunt. They figured he'd jump out of his seat and deliver his familiar line: "Smile! You're on *Candid Camera*!" Created by Funt, who died at 84 of complications from a stroke, the show drew millions of viewers in its 1960s heyday. The secret?

Put regular folks in irregular predicaments, add a soupçon of sadism and enjoy. Funt placed a "guard" at the Delaware state line to tell drivers that Delaware was closed for the day, and had a bank teller selling counterfeit money at a discount. His signature line climaxed each bit, and his genial warmth soothed the show's sheepish victims. The Brooklyn-born son of Russian immigrants launched a prototype on radio in 1947 called *Candid Microphone*. Twice married and divorced, the father of five spent his later years on his ranch in Big Sur, California, still writing and producing the show for syndication. The current show's cohost, Funt's son Peter, provided an epitaph for his provocateur *père*: "He was eternally grateful that people were such good sports."

DeForest Kelley

Trekkies dug his 'Damn it, Jim, I'm just a country doctor!'

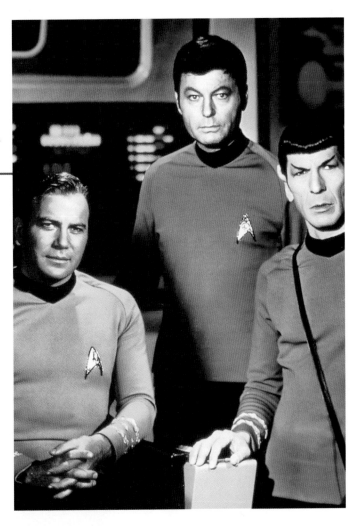

Though he appeared in 150 films and TV shows, DeForest Kelley (center) will best be remembered as Dr. Leonard "Bones" McCoy, the cranky but humane physician, serving faithfully through three TV seasons, decades of reruns and six movie sequels with William Shatner and Leonard Nimoy on *Star Trek*'s USS *Enterprise*. Ironically, Kelley, who died at 79 of stomach cancer, had dreamed as an Atlanta youth of becoming a doctor. When his Baptist minister dad couldn't afford to send him to medical school, Kelley turned to showbiz, where he met Carolyn Dowling, his wife of 54 years. Kelley told the *Houston Chronicle* in 1998 that his major legacy was to "have inspired a great number of people to enter the medical world."

To tell the TRUTH

Peggy Cass

Her wisecracks and warmth made her the definitive TV guest

Peggy Cass (left, with Bud Collyer and Kitty Carlisle Hart) was an accomplished actress more likely to echo in the halls of showbiz history for her gift of brassy-voiced gab. Cass won the 1956 Tony (and later an Oscar nomination) as *Auntie Mame*'s pregnant secretary Agnes Gooch. But with her first appearance on *The Jack Paar Show* in 1958, she later noted, "all of a sudden, I was famous." Until her death from heart failure at 74, Cass played the TV circuit, traveled with her retired teacher husband, Eugene Feeney, and kept up with a wide circle of friends. As one of them, talk show panelmate Orson Bean, recalled, "She was just a joy to be around."

James Farmer

A slave's grandson stood proud on the front lines of the civil rights battle

In the years leading up to his death from congestive heart failure at 79, James Farmer lost his sight and his legs to the ravages of diabetes. It seemed a cruelly ironic fate for a founder of the Congress for Racial Equality who, at the height of the civil rights movement, embodied vision and momentum. In 1942, the same year he cofounded CORE, Farmer, the Texas-born son of a professor, organized one of the early antisegregation sit-ins at a Chicago coffee shop. By 1961 he was leading the first Freedom Rides and soon was literally putting his life on the line in demonstrations that sometimes landed him in southern jails. As CORE became eclipsed by more radical black-power groups, Farmer faded from prominence. In 1968, running as a Republican, he lost a Brooklyn congressional race to Shirley Chisholm. He then

RAISA GORBACHEV

In a Russia swept by change, her love for her husband, and his for her, was constant

As the Soviet Union's first true First Lady, Raisa Gorbachev smashed the babushka mold. During the heady six years of her husband Mikhail's reformist regime, she entranced Westerners —though not her fellow Soviets, who found her too pushy— with her intelligence and self-assured sense of style. "She showed a surprised world that a Russian woman could be tactful, charming and elegant," says Georgy Shakhnazarov, a former adviser of Gorbachev's. Yet the role Raisa cherished most was that of Mikhail's wife. "Everything else in her life took a backseat," says another adviser, Alexander Galkin. Even on her deathbed, she fretted about her husband, grilling their only child, Irina, 42, "What is your father eating? How is he dressed?" Raisa succumbed to leukemia at 67, just five days shy of the couple's 46th wedding anniversary.

In 1964 he was hauled away from a protest at New York's World's Fair.

served briefly as assistant secretary of Health, Educa-tion and Welfare in the Nixon Admin-istration. In recent years the widowed father of two worried about his place in history. "I have had a great anxiety that my people would forget me," he told PEOPLE. Those fears were assuaged in 1998, when he was awarded the Presidential Medal of Freedom.

JOSEPH HELLER
War's madness was his muse

It was the ultimate catch-22: You write a book so seismic that everything subsequent is deemed inferior. Such was the fate of Joseph Heller, whose 1961 debut novel became a World War II classic (and a Mike Nichols film). *Catch-22* told of a bombardier, whose dark shenanigans mirrored Heller's own 60 Air Force missions over Europe. When an interviewer suggested that Heller had never equaled it, the cocky Brooklynite, who died at 76 of a heart attack, snapped, "Who has?" The son of a truck driver, Heller used G.I. benefits to get a master's in lit before writing ad copy, TV and movie scripts as well as six novels. In 1981, after the collapse of his marriage, the father of two was stricken by Guillain-Barré syndrome, a paralyzing, life-threatening nerve disorder, which led to a nonfiction chronicle, *No Laughing Matter,* and remarriage, to the nurse who facilitated his recovery.

LIZ TILBERIS
A fashion editor faced a deadly disease with uncommon style

When Liz Tilberis (left), editor-in-chief of *Harper's Bazaar,* died at 51 after a valiant six-year battle with ovarian cancer, colleagues and friends were stunned. Up to the very end, the down-to-earth British expatriate had worked tirelessly on the magazine she'd revitalized, crusaded for cancer research and made time for husband Andrew and their two teen sons as well as a circle of pals that included Princess Di and Calvin Klein. "Liz came from one place, and that was love," said designer Donna Karan. Added socialite Blaine Trump: "Liz was the snap, crackle and pop of the fashion world."

HARRY BLACKMUN

A conservative appointee wound up the people's judge

"I'll carry this one to my grave," said Supreme Court Justice Harry A. Blackmun, speaking about the landmark 1973 *Roe v. Wade* decision he wrote which effectively legalized abortion. When he died at 90 of complications following hip replacement surgery, Blackmun was also remembered as the down-home jurist who delighted in wiggling his ears for children visiting the court. (Less outgoing otherwise, though, he was called "the shy person's justice" by fellow Minnesotan Garrison Keillor.) Certainly this grocer's son and scholarship student at Harvard seemed an unlikely central figure in perhaps the most heated and intractable political debate of the past quarter century.

He was a Republican appointed by Richard Nixon in 1970 after two earlier nominees were rejected by the Senate. "It always kept me a little on the humble side," said Blackmun, who jokingly referred to himself as Old No. 3. At first his opinions closely followed those of his boyhood friend Chief Justice Warren E. Burger. But over the years Blackmun shifted leftward, which some attributed to the influence of his feminist wife Dorothy and three daughters, others to an alliance with liberal judges Thurgood Marshall and William J. Brennan.

Blackmun later took a dissenting stand against capital punishment, stating that "the death penalty experiment has failed" and that it was a "delusion" to believe it could be applied in anything but a random and arbitrary way. As Chai Feldblum, a Georgetown University law professor and former Court clerk, said, "He never started with the law, he started with the people and how the law might affect them." Blackmun conceded that he had agonized over *Roe,* but that "once a decision has been made, I don't lose sleep over it." A man of principle, he never came to regret that controversial *Roe* opinion despite all the hate mail and death threats he incurred as a result. On his retirement in 1994, Blackmun said, "I think it was right in 1973, and I think it is right today."

AKIO MORITA

His Walkman enabled music lovers to tune out anyone, anytime, anywhere

From the day he was born in 1921 in the industrial city of Nagoya, Japan, there was little doubt what eldest son Akio Morita would do when he grew up. His family, after all, had owned and run a sake business for 14 generations. But one day when young Akio was in junior high school, his family bought a phonograph—a gizmo that so entranced Morita that it would alter his life's path. In 1946 that fascination was rekindled when he saw his business partner Masaru Ibuka wearing headphones to listen to a tape recorder. That gave Morita an idea that, upon its debut in 1979, would change the way the world listened to music: the Sony Walkman.

Morita, who was 78 when he died of pneumonia, personified for Westerners the postwar rise of Japan from defeated warrior to industrial giant. Japan was still reeling when Ibuka invited his old Imperial Navy comrade to join the fledgling electronics company that would come to be named Sony, from *sonus,* the Latin word for sound. Morita went along, but only after gaining his father's permission to abandon the sake business. Sony's first breakthough in 1955, a near-pocket-size radio, was followed by the Trinitron, which was the first reliable color TV, and the ill-fated Betamax VCR. Despite his enormous success, Morita, who had three children with his wife, Yoshiko, lived modestly. His one indulgence: a huge loudspeaker in his living room.

MADELINE KAHN

She lit up stage and screen, both large and small, with her distinctive humor

Her trademark nasal twang and madcap drollery stamped Madeline Kahn as a one-of-a-kind comedian. In a career that spanned four decades, the hilariously funny blonde did it all—TV, Broadway, film—garnering an Emmy and a Tony plus two Oscar nominations. But Kahn, 57, who was featured for three seasons on CBS's *Cosby,* will be best remembered for her off-the-wall screen collaborations with Mel Brooks. Her distinctive turns as a sexually demanding bride in *Young Frankenstein* and a Marlene Dietrichesque saloon singer in *Blazing Saddles* were punctuated with flouncy gestures, wriggling hips and an unforgettable lisping voice. "She was the perfect performer," says Peter Boyle, her *Frankenstein* costar. Diagnosed in September 1998 with ovarian cancer, Kahn, who was intensely private, did not let the public in on her painful secret until one month before her death. Just four weeks earlier, Kahn got married for the first time, to attorney John Hansbury, 49, whom she'd been dating for a decade.

YEHUDI MENUHIN

A child violin virtuoso became an ambassador of international humanity

In 1924, at age 8, Yehudi Menuhin made his professional violin debut playing Bériot's *Scène de Ballet* with the San Francisco Symphony Orchestra. After his New York City premiere two years later, Menuhin, whom violinist Itzhak Perlman hailed as "the most phenomenal child prodigy that ever existed, certainly in this century," joined the circuit of Europe's most celebrated concert halls. By 12, he had embarked on a prolific recording career that would include not only the classical canon and major contemporary works but also jazz and Eastern music, including his "East Meets West" series, which in the 1960s introduced Indian sitarist Ravi Shankar to Western audiences.

Born in New York City, Menuhin was the first of three musically gifted children born to Russian émigrés. By his teens he was recording with his pianist sister Hephzibah, a favorite recital partner for four decades. Knighted in Britain and made an honorary Swiss citizen, Menuhin was a dedicated internationalist who conducted orchestras and nurtured musical talent around the globe. No stranger to controversy, he championed such humanitarian causes as racial equality in South Africa, and sought to melt the Cold War cultural divide by bringing Soviet musicians to play in the U.S. Menuhin, who died at 82 of heart failure after a long dedication to yoga and health food, is survived by his wife of 52 years, dancer Diana Gould, and by four children and four grandchildren.

IRISMURDOCH A terrible disease stilled a powerful writer but not her mate's endless, eloquent love

Iris Murdoch and husband John Bayley shared a literary devotion that matched that of the Brownings, and, indeed, one critic called his 1999 work *Elegy for Iris* "one of the longest love letters ever written." Sadly, though, it chronicled the last chapter of their 43-year union, when Alzheimer's disease gradually diminished Murdoch's powers and then took her life at 79. Choosing not to have children, they concentrated on their distinguished careers. Bayley, 73, is an Oxford don and critic; Murdoch had been a brilliant, prolific writer of philosophical essays, plays and poetry but is best known for her 26 novels, including the prize-winning *The Sea, the Sea* and *The Black Prince*. Their marriage had been a playland, with joyful rituals like skinny-dipping in rivers as boating parties floated by. But Murdoch's illness took hold in the mid-1990s. The doctors seemed to give up but not Bayley, who bathed and fed her, prepared her morning muesli and chatted with her constantly even as her replies made less and less sense. It was only in her final three weeks that he took her to a nursing home a mile from their Oxford cottage. At her side when she died, Bayley later told the newspaper *The Independent,* "She was just smiling at us and being conscious of the fact that we were loving her. She had such a wonderfully good death, so calm."

GEORGE C. SCOTT

A general electric in *Dr. Strangelove* and *Patton,* he turned fury into fame

When he marches in front of a giant American flag to thunder at an unseen audience in the opening moments of the 1970 film *Patton* (left), George C. Scott reduces viewers to quivering boot-camp recruits. Those who were lucky—and unlucky— enough to work with the tempestuous Scott felt equally queasy. Daniel Petrie Sr., who directed him in the 1963-64 TV drama *East Side, West Side,* recalls having to pull over while driving to the set one day to deal with a bout of Scott-induced nausea. Says Petrie: "I was absolutely terrified of him." Though he was recognized as one of the great actors of his time, life for—and with—Scott was hardly a smooth ride. Born in Wise, Virginia, he lost his mother at age 8 and grew up in Detroit, where his father worked for Buick. Scott, who called himself "a functioning alcoholic," began boozing in the late 1940s, when he was a Marine burying bodies at Arlington National Cemetery. He married five times (twice to the late actress Colleen Dewhurst), but his last marriage, to actress Trish Van Devere, worked. He fathered six children (one out of wedlock). The pugnacious Scott had his nose broken half a dozen times in brawls. "He used to have a bodyguard who was there to protect other people from him," recalls Paul Sorvino, his costar in *The Day of the Dolphin.*

Despite his irascibility, Scott, who died at 71 of an aortic aneurysm, charmed the ladies and never bragged. "George was truly one of the greatest and most generous actors I have ever known," said Jack Lemmon, a costar in *Inherit the Wind.* Such courtesy did not extend to the Motion Picture Academy. After failing to win an Oscar for 1959's *Anatomy of a Murder,* he scoffed at future nominations; on the evening he won Best Actor for *Patton,* Scott was in Upstate New York—watching hockey on TV.

SAUL STEINBERG

An inspired émigré
cartoonist made us see
ourselves in a fresh light

He hated being known as "the man who did that poster," but it was his much-imitated satirical *New Yorker* cover (subsequently a poster), featuring a Manhattan-centric *View of the World from 9th Avenue,* that made Saul Steinberg famous. Romanian-born, he trained as an architect in Milan, then fled Fascist Italy and in 1942 arrived in America, where he got the assignment that established his calling. As a Navy ensign he was sent back to Italy to draw Resistance-inspiring cartoons, which were to be dropped behind German lines.

His subsequent work was no less persuasive. Elevating simple doodles into art, Steinberg was "a philosopher in pictorial symbols," says artist Art Spiegelman, and his drawings indelibly altered America's self-image. "You can't remember what you thought of something—like the Manhattan view—before he drew it," says Françoise Mouly, art editor of *The New Yorker,* which published 727 Steinberg drawings, 85 of them on the cover, over five decades. Steinberg adored his adopted land, not least its distinguishing attractions like diners, baseball, motels and the landscapes of the Great Plains. Often considered aloof, Steinberg sometimes posed in a paper mask, explaining that Americans "manufacture a mask of happiness for themselves." He was "a very private person," says his wife, Hedda Sterne, who remained a friend after they separated in the 1970s and was with him when he died of cancer at 84. "He just wanted to draw."

LEO CASTELLI
A dealer, meanwhile,
also an Italian refugee,
was planting our flag atop the world of art

It took a suave Italian expatriate who spoke five languages to convince a snobbish, skeptical world of the importance of postwar American art. By the time of his death at 91, Leo Castelli was the most influential art dealer of his day. "Anyone can discover an artist," he once said, "but to make him what he is, give him importance—that's really discovery." Among the artists he really discovered were Roy Lichtenstein, Frank Stella and the flag-flaunting Jasper Johns. As a result of his skillful diplomacy and advocacy in Europe, they became internationally recognized, and in 1964, another of his protégés, Robert Rauschenberg, became the first American to win the top prize at the Venice Biennale. The cosmopolitan son of a Trieste banker, Castelli had dabbled in the Paris art world before World War II, then fled for the U.S. and gained citizenship after working for Army intelligence. In a notoriously Byzantine business, Castelli, who married three times, was a straightforward, honest man who put artists he believed in on a payroll, regardless of sales. In 1958 he paid $1,200 for *Bed,* a work Rauschenberg had painted on his quilt because he couldn't afford canvas. In 1988, before gifts to institutions were tax-deductible, Castelli donated it to New York City's Museum of Modern Art. Its estimated worth by then was $10 million.

WALTERPAYTON

The legendary running back they called
Sweetness was mourned as a jock and gent

Indisputably, Walter Payton was one of the greatest running backs in grid history. At the time of his retirement in
1987 (below), he was the National Football League's all-
time leading rusher, with 16,726 yards. A fierce competitor,
he missed only one game of the 190 the Chicago Bears played
during his 13-year career—an astonishing feat given the
relentless battering running backs take. Yet Payton was loved
by fans and teammates as much for his playful personality
and gracious character as for his athletic ability. When he
died at 45 in his South Barrington, Illinois, home of a rare
cancer, nine months after announcing he needed a liver trans-
plant (which he did not get), he was surrounded by wife
Connie, 45, and children Jarrett, 18, and Brittney, 14.

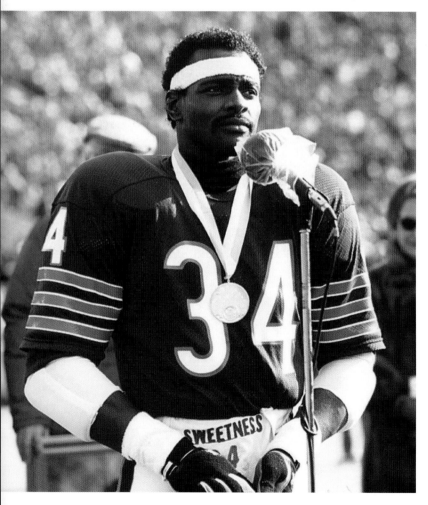

WILT CHAMBERLAIN

He swaggered gaudily through
life and into the NBA Valhalla

At 7'1", he was a towering presence who never failed to amaze. From 1959 to 1973, starring for the Philadelphia Warriors and 76ers and later for the L.A. Lakers, Wilt Chamberlain set dozens of NBA records, including the unthinkable feat of scoring 100 points in a single game. Off the court, he scored as well, clouding his fame with notoriety when he claimed in his 1991 memoir that he had slept with 20,000 women. "Those who know me have no problem with that number," said the never-modest, never-wed Chamberlain, who dismissively told detractors, "Nobody roots for Goliath."

But for fans, the tireless, physically intimidating showman left a legacy of respect. "He's tall and he's strong and he's handsome," his decade-long rival, Bill Russell of the Boston Celtics, once said, "but the most important thing is he's a very intelligent basketball player." In retirement, Chamberlain dabbled in everything from real estate to acting, suffered declining health and was found dead at 63 of an apparent heart attack at his home in Bel Air, California.

Shel Silverstein His poems and drawings enchanted audiences of all ages

Shel Silverstein was that rare contradiction: a recluse totally engaged in life. He so shunned publicity that he refused to let his publisher distribute information about him. Yet he also said, "I want to go everywhere, look at and listen to everything"—and he did. The divorced Silverstein, who left behind a son, Matthew, 15, died of a heart attack in Florida, one of the four states where he had homes. But during a prolific career that spanned five decades, the peripatetic playwright, minstrel and author, 68, left his whimsical mark on Nashville, Hollywood, Broadway and, most indelibly, on the world of children's literature. His dozen books—among them *The Giving Tree, Where the Sidewalk Ends* and the bestselling *A Light in the Attic*—have been translated into 20 languages and have sold some 14 million hardback copies worldwide. Sums up Hugh Hefner, who gave Silverstein his first major break by featuring his cartoons, stories and poems in *Playboy*: "He really was a Renaissance man."

SYLVIA SIDNEY

A '30s screen star was still wowing 'em into her own 80s

"They used to pay me by the teardrop," said redoubtable, thrice-wed actress Sylvia Sidney, who died of throat cancer at 88. In the 1930s she played vulnerable-if-gutsy working girls in such movies as *An American Tragedy* and *Fury.* Then, sick of typecasting, she opted for stage and TV (and needlepoint design), returning to film with an Oscar nomination for *Summer Wishes, Winter Dreams* (1973). Game till the end, she relished roles in Tim Burton's *Beetlejuice* (1988) and *Mars Attacks!* (1996).

KATHRYN MURRAY

A happy hoofer helped turn the U.S. into a ballroom

Kathryn Kohnfelder was just 17 when Arthur Murray, then 29, spotted her in his radio audience and invited her onto the stage to help demonstrate a dance step. Married four months later, the pair built a 500-studio dance-instruction empire and waltzed their way into millions of homes on *The Arthur Murray Party,* which ran variously on each of the three networks between 1950 and 1960. Kathryn, 92, who outlived Arthur by eight years, was a more than equal partner. He got rich, said a wag, "by the sweat of his Frau."

SusanStrasberg

Frankly, this starlet, memoirist and daughter of legends gave a damn, making for a *Bittersweet* life

As a maid of honor in 1994, Susan Strasberg received an embroidered pillow from the bride that read, "Life is uncertain. Eat dessert first." It referred to more than Strasberg's insatiable sweet tooth. The actress, who died of cancer at 60, had been a Broadway sensation playing the title role in *The Diary of Anne Frank* when she was 17. But despite prodigious talent that impressed even her celebrated parents, Method-acting teachers Lee and Paula Strasberg, she never replicated that early success. Her Hollywood career began with acclaim in such films as 1955's *Picnic,* but she drifted into lesser roles and endured a disastrous one-year marriage to fellow actor Christopher Jones in 1965. More memorable than most of her movies were her famous friendships (Marilyn Monroe, who lived for a time with the Strasberg family, was like a sister) and romances with Richard Burton, Warren Beatty and Cary Grant. In later years Strasberg, who had one daughter, told all in two well-written books that dealt frankly with her own insecurities and diminished expectations. "There I was, sitting in Hollywood," she wrote in her 1980 autobiography, *Bittersweet,* "just waiting for someone to want me."

Mario Puzo

After he created The Godfather, even mobsters lined up to shake his hand

Mario Puzo was determined to complete one final Mafia novel despite a weakening heart. "As I finish the last word, I fall over," he joked to Carol Gino, his companion of 20 years. He got his wish. After a visit from his editor, who raved about *Omerta,* he died in bed at 78.

Puzo often said that his real subject was the complicated bonds of family. "I never met a real, honest-to-God gangster," he wrote pre-*Godfather,* but Puzo grew up in Manhattan's notoriously gang-ridden Hell's Kitchen. He was well behaved himself because of his formidable mother, who raised seven children after her railroad-worker husband left. "Whenever the Godfather opened his mouth . . . I heard the voice of my mother," her son wrote. Puzo married Erika Broske, whom he'd met while serving in Germany during World War II, and wrote well-received novels that sold too poorly for the father of five to quit his day jobs. So Puzo decided to hack out the most commercial tome he could, featuring the Italian mobsters he'd heard about as a boy. Published in 1969, *The Godfather* sold 21 million copies and inspired two Oscar-winning movies (which Puzo cowrote). Despite all the hoopla, this modest man kept his modest Long Island home and limited his indulgences to cigars, good food and the occasional gambling jaunt to Las Vegas. "He said that if he ever got to heaven," Carol Gino recalled, "all he'd ask for is a fresh roll with butter every morning."

PICTURE CREDITS

FRONT COVER (JFK Jr) Gregory Heisler/Corbis Outline • (Ricky Martin) Dana Fineman/Corbis Sygma • (Susan Lucci) Frank Veronsky • (Regis Philbin) Carol Friedman/Corbis Outline • (Julia Roberts) Gregory Pace/Corbis Sygma • (Mike Myers) New Line Cinema • (Serena Williams) Chris Trotman/Duomo

BACK COVER (Sophie and Edward) Tim Graham/Corbis Sygma • (Gwyneth Paltrow) Blake Little/Visages • (George C. Scott and Trish Van Devere) Steve Shapiro • (Britney Spears) Jen Lowery/London Features

JFK JR. TRIBUTE 4-5 Luca Bruno/AP; (inset) Mike Segar/Reuters/Archive Photos • 6-7 (clockwise from top left) Laura Cunningham/Globe Photos; Stephen Rose/Liaison Agency; David L. Ryan/The Boston Globe; Chris Erbetta/Corbis Sygma; Rick Friedman/Black Star • 8-9 (clockwise from top left) Evan Agostini/Liaison Agency; Sipa; Stephen Savoia/APWideworld; Les Stone/Corbis Sygma • 10-11 (clockwise from left) Paul Adoa/Corbis Sygma; Laura Cavanaugh/Globe Photos; The Coqueran Group • 12-13 (clockwise from top left) Edinger/Liaison Agency; Dirck Halstead/Liaison Agency; Paul Adao/Corbis Sygma; CBS Photo Archive; Corbis Bettmann-UPI

PEOPLE'S PEOPLE 14-15 J.C./Katz/Corbis Outline • 16 Theo Kingma/Shooting Star • 17 (from top) Lisa Means; Keri Pickett • 18 Michael O'Neil/Corbis Outline • 19 Albert Sanchez/Corbis Outline • 20 George Holz/Corbis Outline • 21 Ruven Afanador/Corbis Outline • 22 (from left) Paul Fenton/Shooting Star; Kathy Hutchins/Hutchins Photo Agency; Gregory Pace/Corbis Sygma • 23 (from left) Rick Mackler/Globe Photos; Kevin Mazur; Evan Agostini/Liaison Agency • 24 Andrew Schwartz/SMPSP • 25 Wes Bell

HEADLINERS 26-27 (from left) Juanito Holandez Jr.; Gary Caskey/Reuters; George Kochaniec/Rocky Mountain News/Corbis Sygma • 28-29 (clockwise from top left) George Kochaniec/Rocky Mountain News/Corbis Sygma; Ed Andrieski/APWideworld; APWideworld; Thomas Michael Alleman; KMGH/APWideworld • 30 (bottom) Liaison Agency • 31 Mary Altaffer • 32-33 Keystone/APWideworld; (inset) Yvain Geneevay/Sipa Press • 34 AFP/Corbis; Corbis/Sygma • 35 (from top) Larry Downing/Reuters/Archive Photos; Peter Morgan/Reuters/Archive Photos; AFP/Corbis • 36-37 (clockwise from left) Jerome Delay/APWideworld; Yannis Kontos/Corbis Sygma; Seamus Conlan; Robert Wallis; Yannis Konto • 38-39 (from left) Mitchel Layton/Duomo; Traver/Liaison Agency; Chris Trotoman/Duomo; Janette Beckman/Corbis Outline; Barton Silverman/NYT Pictures • 40 (from left) Neal Preston/Corbis Outline; Lisa Means • 41 Joel Saget/AFP • 42 Kevin Bennett/Bangor Daily News; APWideworld • 43 (from left) Daryn Slover/Lewiston Sun-Journal/APWideworld; Manuello Paganelli/Corbis Sygma • 44 Focus/Marr • 45 Karin Cooper/Liaison Agency • 46 (from top) Andrea Renault/Globe Photos; Gabe Kircheimer/Black Star • 47 Chip Hires/Liaison Agency • 48-49 (clockwise from left) Sara Corwin; Jonthan Moffat/Zuma Press; Mark Sennet/Reflex • 50 Robin Bowman • 51 Ricki Rosen/Saba • 52 National Science Foundation/APWideworld • 53 (from top) Doug Mills/APWideworld; Jim Mone/APWideworld

PARTY ANIMALS 54-55 Eric Draper/APWideworld; (inset) Lisa Rose/Globe Photos • 56-57 (from left) Ron Davis/ Shooting Star; Eric Draper/APWideworld; Eric Charbonneau/Berliner Studio; Lisa Rose/Globe Photos; Johnson/Hutchins; Fitzroy Bennett/Globe Photos • 58-59 (from left) Steve Granitz/Retna Ltd.; Chris Haston/APWideworld; Berliner Studio; Rose Prouser/Reuters; Ron Wolfson/Online USA; Ron Davis/Shooting Star • 60-61 (from left) Lisa Rose/Globe Photos (2); Tamie Arroyo; Lisa Rose/Globe Photos; Steve Cohen/Berliner Studio; Lisa Rose/Globe Photos • 62 (from left) John Barrett/Globe Photos; Ann Limengello/ABC; courtesy Susan Lucci • 63 Steve Granitz/Retna Ltd. (4) • 64 Frank Micellotta/Image Direct (3) • 65 (from left) Michael Green/APWideworld; Lisa Rose/Globe Photos; Tim Chappell/Reuters • 66 Lisa Rose/Globe Photos (3) • 67 (from top) David Allocca/DMI; Chris Martinez/Reuters

SENSATIONS 68-69 Dana Fineman/Corbis Sygma • 70 (from top) Lynsey Addario/APWideworld; David Bergman/Miami Herald/APWideworld • 71 Lisa Means • 72-73 Robert Beck/Sports Illustrated • 74 (from top) Gregg DeGuire/London Features; Everett Collection • 75 K. Wright/New Line Cinema; (inset) Interfoto/Sipa • 76 Ron Phillips/Spyglass Entertainment Group • 77 Stephanie Cardinale/Corbis Sygma; (inset) Photofest • 78 Anthony Neste/HBO; (inset) Everett Collection • 79 (from top) Evan Kafka; Maria Melin/AC • 80 Everett Collection; (inset) Neal Peters Collection • 81 (top) Anna Summa/Liaison Agency; (inset) Everett Collection; (bottom) Monty Brinton/CBS; (inset) CBS Photo Archives • 82-83 (from left) Black/Toby; Kevin Mazur • 84 Alison Leach; Steve Labadessa • 85 Ron Wolfson/London Features • 86 (top) James Kegley, © Nintendo USA • 87 Rafael Fuchs • 88 Kevin Lamarque/Reuters/Archive • 89 Scott Olson/Reuters/Achive

FAMILY MATTERS 90-91 Tim Graham/Corbis Sygma • 92 Lionel Cironneau/AP • 93 Geoff Wilkinson • 94-95 (clockwise from top left) APTV/APWideworld; Blue (2); Ian Jones/FSP/Liaison Agency; Ian Cook • 96 (from left) Michael Tamaro/APWideworld; Lawrence Schwartzwald/Corbis Sygma • 97 (clockwise from top) Greg Smith/Saba; Alberto Tolot; Andrea Renault/Globe Photos • 98 (clockwise from top right) Andrea Renault/Globe Photos; Frank Trapper/Corbis Sygma; Lisa Rose/Globe Photos; Fitzroy Barrett/Globe Photos • 99 (clockwise from top left) Alex Olivera/Startraks; Mirek Towski/DMI; Darren Fletcher/Express Syndication • 100 (clockwise from top right) Mark Sennet/Reflex; courtesy Mickelson Family; Lisa Rose/Globe Photos • 101 (clockwise from top left) Alex Berliner; All Action/Retna Ltd.; Jeff Christiansen/Liaison Agency • 102 (clockwise from top left) Crescenzo G.P. Notarile; Lisa Rose/Globe Photos; Jim Smeal/Galella Ltd. • 103 (clockwise from top left) Jim Smeal/Galella Ltd.; courtesy Lizzie Grubman PR; Jim Smeal/Galella Ltd.; Deborah Feingold/Corbis Outline • 104 (clockwise from top right) Steve Connolly/Photolink; Ken Regan/Camera 5; Richard Young/Rex USA • 105 (clockwise from top left) John Spellman/Retna Ltd.; APWideworld; Arnal/Geral/Stills/Retna Ltd. • 106 (clockwise from top left) Jim Smeal/Galella Ltd.; Tammie Arroyo/IPOL; Lucy Atkins/San Francisco Examiner; Gilbert Flores/Celebrity Photo • 107 (clockwise from top left) Robin Platzer/Twin Images; Lisa Rose/Globe Photos; Adam Scull/Globe Photos

TRIBUTE 108-109 Hy Peskin/Life magazine • 110 (from top) Photofest; Corbis/Bettmann • 111 Ann States/Saba • 112-113 (clockwise from left) DeBorchgrave/Liaison Agency; John Swappell/Camerapress/Retna Ltd.; Chuck Kennedy/IPOL • 114 SMP/Globe Photos • 115 Philip Guarisco • 116 Everett Collection • 117 Culver Pictures • 118 Photofest • 119 (from top) ScreenScenes; Patrick Harbron/Corbis Outline • 120 Kobal Collection • 121 Everett Collection • 122 CBS Photo Archives • 123 (from top) ScreenScenes; CBS Photo Archives • 124 Anthony Camerano/APWideworld • 125 Despotivic/Corbis Sygma • 126 (from top) Thomas Victor; Thomas Lau/Corbis Outline • 127 © Doug Chevalier/The Washington Post • 128 Deborah Feingold/Corbis Outline • 129 Maddy Miller • 130 Icono/Sipa Press • 131 Express Newspapers/Archive Photos • 132-133 (from left) MPTV; Columbia Pictures/Archive Photos • 134 Malcolm Kirk • 135 Eliot Elisofon/Life magazine • 136 Bill Smith • 137 Brian Lanker • 138 Alice Ochs/Michael Ochs Archives • 139 Everett Collection (2) • 140 Everett Collection • 141 Ken Schles/Corbis Outline